T h e

POISON

IVY,
OAK &
SUMAC
BOOK

DATE DUE

EDERA TRIFOLIA CANADENSIS.

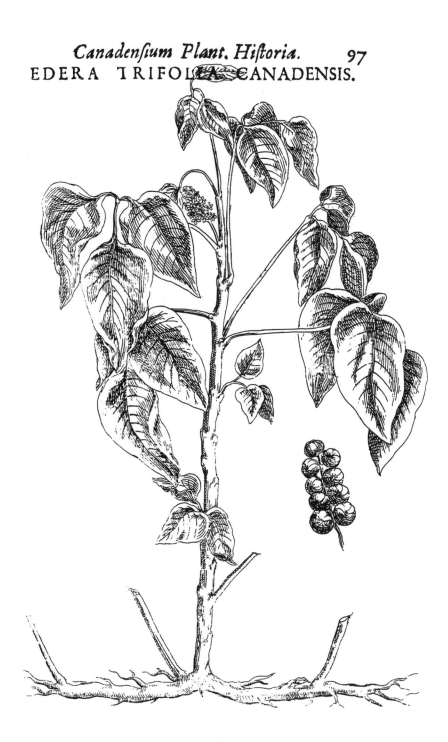

The

POISON

IVY, OAK & SUMAC

BOOK

A Short Natural History and Cautionary Account

Thomas E. Anderson

ACTON CIRCLE
Ukiah, California

The Poison Ivy, Oak & Sumac Book:
A Short Natural History and Cautionary Account

Published by
Acton Circle Publishing Company
P.O. Box 1564
Ukiah, CA 95482

Copyright © 1995 by Thomas E. Anderson
Cover and Interior Design: Lisa Berman
Printed and bound in the United States of America by BookCrafters, Inc.

Published May 1995
8 7 6 5 4 3 2 1

Publisher's Cataloging in Publication
Anderson, Thomas E.
The poison ivy, oak & sumac book: a short natural history and
cautionary account / Thomas E. Anderson.
Includes bibliographical references and index.
p. cm.
ISBN 0-9639371-8-9
1. Poison ivy   2. Poison oak   3. Poison sumac
4. Poisonous plants.   I. Title.
SB618.P6A551 1995   581.6'9   95-75276

Printed on recycled paper.

ACKNOWLEDGMENTS

This book was far from a solo undertaking. I have imposed on and am indebted to numerous gifted people whose generosity is the source of whatever insight and instruction appear in it.

First, I wish to thank William L. Epstein, M.D., of Dermatology Research at the University of California Medical School, San Francisco, for his valuable and liberal assistance in addressing the medical intricacies of this subject. I wish also to thank Douglas Puckering of Mendocino Community College for subjecting the manuscript to his broad knowledge of practically everything. This book would have been much the poorer without the contributions of their time and knowledge; any remaining errors of fact or interpretation are mine alone.

My special thanks go also to: Vera S. Byers, M.D., of U.C. Medical School, San Francisco; Alan Chovil, M.D., Director of Communicable Disease Control, Santa Barbara County, California; Sarah

Colusni of the American Academy of Allergy and Immunology, and Vincent Beltrani, M.D., of its Committee on Contact Dermatitis; Mahmoud A. ElSohly, of the Research Institute of Pharmaceutical Sciences at the University of Mississippi; Dan L. Brown, of the Department of Animal Sciences, Cornell University; Janet McDonald and Lorrie Harrison, of the United States Food and Drug Administration; Judy L. Murphy of the National Institute of Allergy and Infectious Diseases; Glenys A. Rickaby of the Royal Society; Miss J. Vine of the Royal Horticultural Society; Sylvia Bender at the California Department of Mines and Geology Library; Claudia Israel of the Clark Memorial Museum in Eureka, California; Gary Hoshide and Dick Mangan of the United States Forest Service's Equipment Development Center; Tony Schulz of United Catalysts, Inc.; Bob Pomrenke of Miles Laboratories, Pharmaceutical Division; Robert L. Smith, of Tec Laboratories; Jane Higgins-Nelson of Syntex Corporation; Nancy C. Coile of the Florida Department of Agriculture and Consumer Affairs; Dick Otterstad of Otterstad's Brush Control Service in Albany, California; the Asthma & Allergy Foundation; Yvonne Sligh and her staff at the Mendocino Community College Library; the entire North Bay Cooperative Reference Center in Santa Rosa, California; Toni Matsu in Marblehead, Massachusetts; and Denise Kerner, former proprietor of the St. Charles Saloon in Columbia, California.

I am very indebted to Lisa Berman, who designed the cover and these pages, and to Irene Stein, who drafted many of the illustrations.

I wish also to thank Peter Stearns of Ukiah, California, for his fine photographs of western poison oak and his thoughtful views on the place of wild plants in our lives.

Finally, my greatest debt is to Dori, my wife, not only for her undaunted excursions into cyberspace to uncover the minutiae of this eerie subject, but—as in all other endeavors—for her support during my pursuit of it.

T.E.A.
Ukiah, California, 1995

ILLUSTRATIONS

Cover
Poison ivy (*Toxicodendron radicans*) vining on wall. D. Newman (VISUALS UNLIMITED)

Color photo section
AUTHOR
St. Charles Saloon and Poison Oak Show contest entries.

VISUALS UNLIMITED
Poison sumac (*Toxicodendron vernix*) leaf and flowers. Robert Gustafson.
Poison sumac (*T. vernix*) leaf shape. John D. Cunningham.
Poison sumac (*T. vernix*) in fall. John Sohlden.
Eastern poison oak (*Toxicodendron toxicarium, quercifolium* or *pubescens*). Dale Jackson.
Poison ivy (*Toxicodendron radicans*) leaves. John D. Cunningham.
Poison ivy (*T. radicans*), spring. John D. Cunningham.
Poison ivy (*T. radicans*), fall. Dick Thomas.
Poison ivy (*T. radicans*) vine, winter. George Loun.
Poison ivy (*T. radicans*) berries. Jack M. Bostrack.
Rydberg poison ivy (*Toxicodendron rydbergii*) leaves. Doug Sokell.
Rydberg poison ivy (*T. rydbergii*), summer. Doug Sokell.
Rydberg poison ivy (*T. rydbergii*), fall. Doug Sokell.

Pacific/western poison oak (*Toxicodendron diversilobum*), lobed leaves. John D. Cunningham.
Pacific/western poison oak (*T. diversilobum*), late summer. E.F. Anderson.

PETER STEARNS
Pacific/western poison oak (*T. diversilobum*), fall.
Pacific/western poison oak (*T. diversilobum*) in redwood grove.

Black and white illustrations
Poison Oak Show handbill, courtesy of the ST. CHARLES SALOON

IRENE STEIN
Graph of sensitivity to poison ivy, oak, and sumac.
Poison ivy *(Toxicodendron radicans).*
Poison ivy *(T. radicans),* verrucosum.
Poison ivy *(T. radicans),* eximium.
Poison ivy *(T. radicans)* leaf variations.
Poison ivy and oak catechols (two drawings).
The immune response (three drawings)
Cashews.
Mangos.

Common or broadleaf plantain, buckhorn plantain, and jewelweed: Spencer, Edwin Rollin, *All about weeds* (originally published as *Just Weeds* by Charles Scribners & Sons (New York, 1940), Dover Publications reprint, 1966, by permission. Illustrations at pages 157, 237, and 241 by Emma Bergdolt.

Pacific/western poison oak (*Toxicodendron diversilobum*): Parsons, Mary Elizabeth, *The Wild Flowers of California* (Cunningham, Curtis & Welch, 1907), Dover Publications reprint. Illustration at page 9 by Margaret Warriner Buck.

Maps of the range of the poison ivies, oaks and sumac. Crooks, Donald, et al., *Poison Ivy, Poison Oak, and Poison Sumac* (Washington, DC, U.S. Government Printing Office, rev. ed., 1978).

Other leaf, flower, and fruit illustrations: Sargent, Charles Sprague, *Manual of the Trees of North America (Exclusive of Mexico)* (Boston, MA, Houghton-Mifflin, 1905).

Small hydraulic mining operation: Nordhoff, Charles, *California: For Health, Pleasure, and Residence; a book for travellers and settlers* (New York, Harper & Bros., 1872).

CONTENTS

Contents

1
FIRST THINGS:
OBSERVANCE & MISADVENTURE

2
A SOCIAL HISTORY

3
TOXICODENDRON PIE

4
URUSHIOL DERMATITIS

1

God in His wisdom made the fly
And then forgot to tell us why.

—Ogden Nash, "The fly"

FIRST THINGS:
OBSERVANCE &
MISADVENTURE

OLUMBIA, California, in the foothills of the Sierra Nevada mountains has survived the Gold Rush, fires, vandalism, and time. When it burned down in 1857, townspeople rebuilt it in brick with iron fire doors and held on. It is a real place, not a ghost town half-resuscitated, half-invented by the State Parks and Recreation Department. The same breed of people has lived there continuously since the 1850s. From 1945, however, when they accepted the state's offer to preserve the town's character, they have also had to survive their benefactor's good intentions. Parks and Recreation tends to seize and restore any likely edifice within its grant to its original purity, then seal it away from commerce. Columbia's typical public event nevertheless remains resolutely commercial.

Denise Kerner, proprietor of the St. Charles Saloon on the corner of Jackson and Main Streets, said Columbia's first Poison Oak Show in 1982, arose out of an ongoing debate about who had the worst tasting water from local wells. It was a subject that cried out for public airing and judgment. Fittingly, Columbia is just south of Calaveras County where the athleticism of frogs is compared by a similar public review. Poison oak judging was included in the first festival to lend a wider appeal. In time, owing to its popularity, the merits of the poison oak soon prevailed over water's as the subject of public adjudication, although no one recalls how the change occurred.

On the fourth Sunday of every September since that first festival, contestants have sought prizes in such categories as the best arrangement of poison oak, the most potent looking green leaves, the most potent looking red leaves, the biggest single leaf, the best bonsai poison oak, the biggest branch or trunk, and the best photo of poison oak. Entry forms carry a disclaimer:

> **WARNING:** Poison Oak is a poisonous plant. Almost all of us are sensitive to it. ENTER THIS SHOW AT YOUR OWN RISK! If you are fool enough to enter, the St. Charles Saloon takes no responsibility. Children, people who can't be careful, those who know they are very sensitive to poison oak and anyone who enjoys filing lawsuits, should not enter.

Tables outside the saloon soon filled with entries. Handlers trimmed and arranged branches of poison oak, fussed with the arrangements, moved them around for better exposure, and encouraged the electorate to decide among them. Asked whether he was insensitive to poison oak, the chief handler and poll watcher said, "Why, no," and displayed a spot or two of blistering above the wrist. The teenage assistant handler, asked if *he* was insensitive to the plants' oils, responded no and showed his nascent rash. Hugs were preceded with inquiries whether the other party had washed off first. It was a festival of watchful enjoyment.

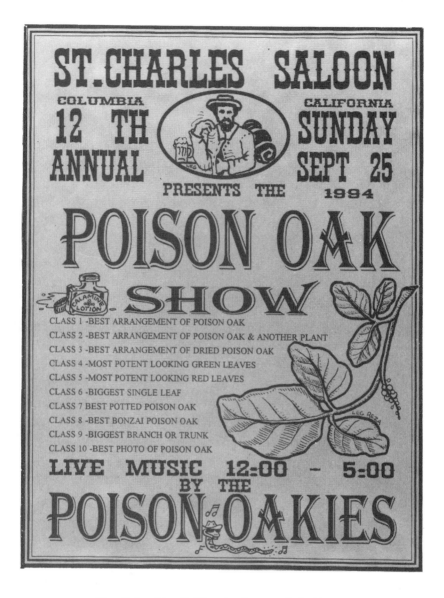

The Columbia, California, Poison Oak Show.

Above the tables were framed 6" to 8" leaflets, and a peace symbol of red leaflets with white berries. Balloting, of the vote-early-and-often variety, continued from noon until the handlers could elicit no further response from the crowd. Prizes were awarded, the band played lustily, and pleasure was almost unlimited.

Poison oak has always been a familiar but never wholly congenial neighbor in the Sierras. The plant impeded many a Forty-Niner's pursuit of fortune and delayed construction of the western stretch of the transcontinental railroad in 1863-1866 with rashes among its work crews.

In May 1968, within a few hundred miles of Columbia, a 55-year-old airline pilot realized his retirement dream: a small ranch, a horse, dogs, and a middle-sized herd of docile Herefords. From almost his first day on the ranch, however, he got poison oak rashes. He remembered once having ridden his horse through areas of poison oak accompanied by his dogs. He continued to pick up the oleoresin and to get rashes from his horse, his saddle, his dogs, almost any animate or inanimate object that contacted the shrub. In September he got an unusually severe case, which his physician treated with a placebo grade poison-oak derived extract to be taken orally in increasing doses, up to nine drops daily. He stopped the treatment in a few days, however, because his rash worsened. In December he developed edema and in March 1969 suffered kidney failure, whereupon he was admitted to the University of California Hospital in San Francisco. The hospital discharged him a month later and with a prescription of corticosteroids to be taken every other day. Despite medication, the lesions on his kidneys failed to heal. His health continued to decline, and in February 1970 he died.

Death from kidney failure is fortunately rare among poison oak, ivy, and sumac victims. By 1975, only 12 known cases had been reported. Biopsies of the skin and kidneys of this patient, however, revealed something never before detected. Circulating antibodies to poison-oak antigens apparently had combined with them to lodge in massive concentrations in the tissues of his skin and kidneys. Death was concluded to be from "immune-complex" nephritis (kidney inflammation), caused when an antigen-antibody combination attaches to and assaults the organ's tissues. Although the rash had subsided when the biopsies were taken, doctors hypothesized that increasing doses of the oils, by both contact and swallowing antitoxin, reinforced a genetic tendency and induced excess production of the antibodies. The biopsies have been frozen for study later when the process is better understood.

ALL-AMERICAN FLORA

Toxicodendron, the poisonous tree, better known as poison ivy, oak, or sumac, is a genus that has vexed North Americans since the first footloose band of us wandered down from the land bridge where the Bering Strait is now. They warned the rest of us, though much good it did. The plants now flourish as they never did before. Besides being troublesome, they and everything about them, are cloaked in contradiction, confusion, and superstition.

They are not ivies or oaks, and are in a different genus from sumacs. Their resinous oils—which cause the rash—are not poisons or even irritants. Practically no other animal is susceptible to them; some even dine on the berries and leaves with relish. The oils don't vaporize to afflict from a distance, but people need not touch the plants to get the rash. Their oils transfer readily from tools, pets, clothes, or anything that touched them first. They last on tools and clothing for months or years. Droplets of the oil in smoke are especially vicious, attacking skin, eyes, nose, throat, and lungs. Poison ivy vines on firewood are double-barreled. If handling doesn't cause a reaction, the oil in the smoke will. Airborne or not, a poison ivy-oak-sumac rash always sneaks up. It appears 24 to 48 hours after contact, but it may delay 72 hours or, in rare first encounters, show up after a few weeks. There's plenty of time to forget the meeting and to spread the oil all over oneself and one's hapless companions. The affected skins then itch, redden, and get tiny blisters that soon enlarge, coalesce, burst, weep, and peel. The last stage hangs on for about four days before the skin crusts over. Then the whole affliction may take two the three weeks to fade slowly away—with luck. A poison ivy, oak, sumac response is rarely systemic, except for those who medicine calls the "exquisitely" sensitive. It can be thoroughly disabling, however, especially when around the eyes, or on the legs and groin to inhibit walking.

Worse, even though each plant's oils differ slightly, poison ivy, oak, or sumac rashes cross-sensitize their victims not only to the other two but to all the harmful species of what is called the Cashew Family. It is a worldwide group that includes cashews, mangoes, the oriental lacquer and Brazilian pepper trees, and several hundred noxious members of the family. Most are tropical or subtropical, and harmless, but mangoes and lacquer ware won't be the fun they used to be. Neither will a tramp through the woods or a morning among (one thought) the roses.

The prerequisite to a rash is developing an *immune response* to the oil. Usually, nothing happens on the first contact or occasionally the first few; it requires an initial preparation. The oil penetrates the skin's thin, hard surface and combines with inner skin tissue proteins. White blood cells go to the site and prepare the body for a future response. Even with this sensitizing contact there is a 5-6 day lull before a response is ready. The typical rash delays 24 to 48 hours after the next contact because it takes that long to organize the response. One side effect (as if one is needed) is that the rash sometimes seems to spread to other parts of the body. One guess is that white cells carry *quinones*, into which urushiol oxidizes once inside the skin, to other slightly irritated skin areas or the sites of old rashes.

Between 75 and 85 percent of all humans are potentially allergic to poison ivy, oak, and sumac. They will get a rash with an adequate dose. About 50 percent can get it from a normal brush with the plants or secondhand. Of the 50 percent who will *not* break out from the normal encounter, about half are moderately sensitive and will react to an above-normal exposure. Only 15 to 25 percent may be truly insensitive.

In the late 1970s the United States Forest Service, a major sponsor of research into the problem, helped confirm figures for sensitivity in the population. In its effort to reduce the plants' casualties among forest workers, particularly fire fighters, the Service retained as consultants William L. Epstein, M.D., a dermatologist and leading poison ivy and oak specialist, and Vera S. Byers, M.D., an immunobiologist, both at the University of California, San Francisco. UCSF is one of a network of Asthma and Allergic Disease Centers around the

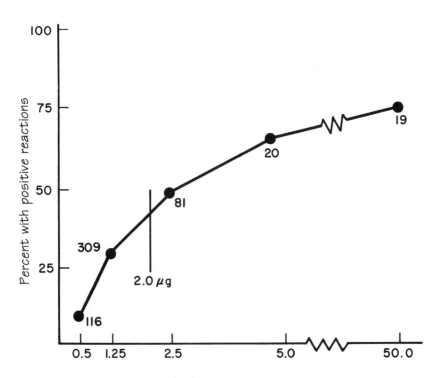

Sensitivity per microgram (μg) of oil, with number tested on the curve.

country. In 1984, to measure sensitivity to the plants, Epstein and Byers designed what resembled a TB patch test. It involved applying standard drops of the oil diluted at strengths of 0.5, 1.25, 2.5, 5.0 and 50 micrograms per drop on people's inner arms. At the end of 48 to 72 hours they read and graded the intensity of each spot's reaction.

About 15 to 25 percent of the subjects tested were insensitive and did not react even to 50 micrograms, 25 times the normal dose. About half the subjects, 25 to 50 percent, were *clinically* sensitive to the oil. They would break out from the average dose, 2.0 micrograms, or an encounter with roughly one crushed leaf. Another 25 to 35 percent were only mildly, or "subclinically," sensitive and needed more than 2.0 micrograms to react. They can become clinically sensitive later in life. Within the clinically sensitive group were the "exquisitely" sensitive—10 to 25 percent—who reacted very intensely to less than 1.0 microgram and would require a doctor's care if exposed to the plant. The patch test kit contained a small tube of cortisone to treat the rash.

ANOTHER NATIONAL PASTIME

As allergenic annoyances, poison ivy, oak, and sumac are more pervasive a part of American life than casual observation suggests.

They are common and frequent gate crashers. According to a *Parenting* magazine article, the adult members of a Fourth of July 1993 wedding party that gathered in Kansas from around the country broke out with unaccountable allergic rashes on their arms and shoulders after they all went home. There was poison ivy in the area. It is everywhere in the U.S.—except for Alaska, Hawaii, and Nevada—below about 5,000 feet elevation. But no one had seen or contacted any. So they decided that pesticides, insects, and detergents were the cause. About two weeks after the adults had become covered in itchy swollen patches (there were no telltale blisters), two young boys in the party broke out. One boy's pediatrician correctly diagnosed poison ivy as the cause, and the adults then recalled hoisting the children on their shoulders to see the fireworks. Later inquiries revealed that earlier in the day the boys had been tumbling downhill into a small patch of the weed.

Poison ivy was the cause of at least one prison break when James W. Worley "voluntarily" left the Richland County, South Carolina, Work Camp in June 1972. Worley had contracted a severe poison ivy rash on his forearm. It caused swelling and eventually weeping sores. A camp official gave Worley calamine lotion. Three times Worley asked to see a doctor but, when denied, he poured Clorox bleach on the sores to relieve the pain. When that proved unsatisfactory, and fearing that he was "in danger of serious bodily harm," as he later told the judge, he left the camp for medical assistance—in Georgia. A doctor there successfully treated the condition with a shot and some medicine. Two years later Worley, still at large, was arrested in Florida and sent back to South Carolina.

At his prison-break trial he raised a defense of "necessity," based on a lack of proper medical treatment. The court remarked that leaving prison might be all right to avoid a serious medical emergency like death or permanent bodily harm, but even then it insisted on an eight-point standard, including surrendering to authorities right after treatment. Worley, who failed on this count, was sent back to camp.

Efforts to overcome the oils' ravages often start in childhood and end in futility. Doctor Harry Lowenburg, Jr., of Philadelphia wrote in the September 13, 1947, *Journal of the American Medical Association* of an 11-year-old boy who had been his patient since 1942 and who in 1946 was admitted to the hospital near death, with a high fever, abnormal breathing, and severe gastro-intestinal symptoms, including wine-red vomit. Given emergency treatment, the boy recovered and was discharged.

By questioning the boy's parents, Dr. Lowenburg learned that for seven weeks before the attack the boy had been swallowing daily doses of a commercial poison-ivy tincture to build up a resistance. To hasten the process he had decided on his own to increase the dose from five to 57 drops daily, nearly four times the manufacturer's recommended adult dosage. Despite his efforts, the boy got two severe attacks of ivy poisoning within a year of the episode anyway.

Many Americans—primarily forest workers, utility line installers, and farmers and ranchers—confront the plants at work. An article in *Audubon* magazine noted a gardener in Connecticut who was cutting poison ivy vines with a knife, which he put away when finished. Several days later, while using the knife for another task, he absently put the blade in his mouth. The lining of the mouth and nose swelled so much that it threatened to impair his breathing. Only quick medical treatment prevented serious harm. In England—where the plants were imported for their brilliant fall foliage—a gardener who had been making cuttings for propagation, was reported kept in the hospital for several months by the "almost corrosive" effects of the sap. The report added with characteristic imperturbability: "There is one other property of this remarkable plant to which attention may be drawn. This is the indelibility of its juice when applied to linen. It produces a quite ineradicable stain, and is, in fact, one of the best possible marking inks available."

Others manage to encounter it at play. *New Yorker* journalist Berton Roueché wrote of a golfer who developed a rash from picking up his ball in the rough after it had taken a single bounce into and out of an adjacent patch of poison ivy. "Why," he queried, "was the golfer picking up his ball in the rough? To improve his lie? Then he deserved what he got." A near relative of the author's, a great woodsman, whittled a collection of twigs for a family wiener roast one summer. He threw the leaves and bark on the fire to flavor the meal. The twigs were poison oak, of course, to which he did not react, although it was an outing the rest of the family will not forget.

THE STANDARD DELUSIONS

Different reactions from seemingly similar contacts; outbreaks from no apparent contact at all; rashes that seem to spread; perceived "cures" from offbeat juices, salves, and powders—these and more create a cloud of mystery around the plants that resists facts like an ozone shield. A handful from the common storehouse includes:

Some people get a rash just standing near the plants. A fallacy that never dies! The nearest thing to vapors from the plants is windborne pollen, which, lacking the gummy reactive oils, is harmless. The oils themselves are among the heaviest, least volatile in the plant kingdom. Even if burned, they do not vaporize but ride around on smoke. A hot summer's day does no more than make half-naked, sweaty people a better target.

Scratching the blisters spreads the rash. Wrong. It can cause and worsen an *infection*, but there are no oils in the harmless, watery ooze from blisters to spread the rash. Initially there may be residual oils not washed off the skin to spread around. The oil takes longer to penetrate thicker parts of the skin, and later eruptions from the same contact may seem like spreading. New contacts from the same or a different source will also start later reactions. Finally, see the above about quinones and flare-ups at the sites of old attacks.

Eating new spring leaflets builds a resistance. This could be a first-class ticket to the emergency room. NEVER DO IT unless absolutely certain you are among the 15 to 25 percent who are insensitive to the oils, in which case you don't need to do it.

Bathing spreads the rash. No, wash. The first thing to do is get the oils off; it is also the second, third, and fourth thing. Plenty of cold running water is handiest and best. Strong laundry soap or detergent, alcohol, and other organic solvents (that won't absolutely fry the skin) also fill the bill. Removing the oil inside one minute could prevent a reaction altogether. Washing with organic solvents within four hours afterward will help. As for irritating the skin, consider its alternative, the rash. Once a rash starts, soothe it with cold compresses and calamine lotion. Stop when the skin peels. Then use moisturizing creams afterwards to relieve the itch. Guard against infection.

Wear rubber gloves when handling it. Bad choice. Rubber dissolves the oil and merely delays its trip to your epidermis. Tight gloves will hold it against the skin and promote the rash. Use heavy leather or cotton gloves. Discard or wash them later with strong soap or detergent.

The rash is temporary; wait it out and it goes away by itself. True enough, but if it affects the eyes, genitals, or more than one fifth of the body; or if nausea, dizziness, or other internal symptoms occur; or if there is no improvement in a few weeks, see a doctor fast.

Science will cure this pestilence. Maybe. Science has been doing its usual good job, but allergies are tricky. Relief—a control, not a cure—may be in sight. Right now, however, the only sure fix is to recognize and avoid the plants, something easier said than done.

GETTING TO KNOW THEM

Plant identification as counseled in song and verse is not entirely helpful. The universally quoted rhymes about poison ivy and oak,

> Leaflets three, let it be,

or (to distinguish it from Virginia creeper)

> Leaves three, leave it be,
> Leaves five, let it thrive,

also

> Leaves of three, quickly flee,
> Berries white, poisonous sight,

more fully rendered as

> Berries red, have no dread,
> Berries white, poisonous sight,
> Leaves three, quickly flee,

are folk sayings. No one knows where they came from, but they probably arose very soon after the colonists' first meeting with the plants. Poison ivy and oak, consistent with their deceptive nature, often produce five, seven, or up to 17 leaflets per leaf.

So much for simple verses. There is more to these desperados than can be summed up in a catchy rhyme. Or in one book. A better understanding may begin, however, with a look at their long, if uninvited, association with us.

2

This tree is not known for its good qualities.
—Peter Kalm, TRAVELS IN AMERICA

A SOCIAL HISTORY

PINIONS about the nature
of poison ivy, oak, and possibly sumac, are divided by, among other
things, the Atlantic Ocean. The first and most notable written statement on the issue is from Captain John Smith (1580-1631). In the
fifth book of his *Generall Historie of Virginia, New England, and the
Summer Isles* (1624) he adjudged that

> The poysoned weed is much in shape like our
> English Ivy, but being but touched, causeth rednesse,
> itching, and lastly blisters, the which howsoever after
> a while passe away of themselves without further
> harme; yet because for the time they are somewhat
> painfull, it hath got it selfe an ill name, although
> questionless of no ill nature.

ON NATIVE GROUNDS AND NOT

No Americans, not even the earliest, were ever so charitable. Onondagas called it *ko-hoon-tas*, stick that makes you sore. Cherokees tried appeasement, addressing it as "my friend." In some languages its name was equivalent to "bad sex" or "venereal disease." The Pomos of northern California expressed mixed feelings at best about Pacific or western poison oak with the name *Ma-tu'-yä"-ho*, "southern fire doctor." And Alma R. Hutchens in her *Indian herbalogy of North America* refers to five plants the Chippewa used to alleviate the rash's symptoms but reported no good word or ritual concerning the plants themselves. Other observers, however, show a better than willing suspension of disbelief about the subject. One from California states that

> More particularly among the northern tribes, the supple slender stems [of poison oak] were used for the warp or ground in woven baskets. The leaves were used by the Karok Indians of northwestern California to cover the bulbs of Soap Root, *Chlorogalum pomeridianum*, while baking them in the earth oven for food. . . . The Concow Indians of Marysville Buttes mixed the leaves into their acorn meal when baking bread, and other tribes used them to spit salmon steaks while they were being smoked.

This report is not unique. Tales of spitting salmon on poison oak appear regularly in other accounts of native uses. No recent source confirms the plant's culinary roles, which seem in any event to have become unfashionable, nor have we found a museum that claims to own a basket with poison oak, either as fiber or a source of dye. Since even centuries-old poison ivy or oak in herbariums has caused rashes, they should be identifiable enough. In fact, there may be no basis for these accounts, except perhaps the credulity of some re-searchers and a better sense of humor than they gave their informants credit for.

One source of the basket story may be a confusion of western poison oak with the splints of one or another variety of squaw bush, which artisans in southern tribes often worked into baskets. Squaw bush (*Rhus trilobata*), also called skunkberry, is a benign relative of poison oak found in the canyons and washes of California's interior valleys. It has sweet red berries and does not cause a rash. In the south the branches were debarked and skillfully split into several strands for wrapping around deer grass to make coiled baskets. Pomos in the north may have used squaw bush as a foundation to weave on, but its use was commoner in the south.

Many tribal cultures did give poison ivy and oak a medicinal status which slightly resembles modern homeopathic practice. The Potawatomi, Meskwaki, and Ojibwa, for example, reportedly used it to cure warts and other blemishes, as did Pomos, according to V. L. Chestnut's *Plants Used by the Indians of Mendocino County*:

> The wart was either cut off close to the base or pricked or cut several times, and the fresh juice was applied immediately. The application had to be repeated several times before the wart would disappear. This juice was also used as a cure for ringworm. Fresh leaves bound together over the bite of a rattlesnake were thought to counteract the poison, but this had to be done immediately.

There is other evidence that some tribes used poison ivy and oak for poultices to open and drain boils, as a disinfectant for open wounds, and an herb against chills, asthma, gonorrhea, tuberculosis, ulcers, and herpes. Poison ivy was thought briefly in 18th-Century England to cure herpes when a case of it disappeared along with a poison ivy rash. Pacific Coast Miwoks rubbed a paste of poison oak charcoal onto their skin before puncturing it to make tattoos. Other than these limited and wary uses, however, legends of a carefree intimacy with poison oak and ivy appear to suggest only a sly joke on prying Europeans.

Early French Canadians named poison ivy *herbe de la puce*, "flea's grass [or wort]," or *bois de chien*, "dog wood." Spanish missionaries in California complained that western poison oak's sap stained their white cassocks indelibly black, and the soldiers accompanying them called it *yiedra de la flecha*, "arrow ivy," or *yiedra maligna*, which needs no translation. But while John Smith's tolerant view found little if any support in North America, it did gain a following in Europe, where the plants were imported soon after he wrote. The eighth edition of W.J. Bean's *Trees & Shrubs Hardy in the British Isles* (1976) notes poison ivy as desirable for the beautiful red tints of its autumn foliage, although it warns fanciers to handle it carefully and plant it out of the way of innocent visitors. The first poison ivy seems to have arrived in Great Britain in 1632, sent by the second John Tradescant.

Captain John Smith

There were three John Tradescants—father, son, and grandson—who were gardeners to the monarchy beginning in 1611. Apparently unruffled by regicide, civil war, the Commonwealth, and the Restoration, the Tradescants not only carried on at their calling but managed to launch British plant collecting in earnest and help found the nursery trade. Their own garden in London listed 1,600 plants in 1656. The first John Tradescant began gathering specimens from North Africa to Archangel in Russia. The second John collected in the Virginia colony, from which he sent home the seeds of the poison ivy.

One of the first British gardeners on record to cultivate the new wonder was Henry Compton, Bishop of London from 1675 to 1713. A nephew of the Duke of Northampton, Compton had the means and will to be the preëminent British collector of exotics in the late 17th and early 18th Centuries. Upon Charles II's restoration to the throne, Compton abandoned his youthful career as a mercenary soldier in Flanders and returned home to be ordained. His connections enabled him shortly after that to attain the bishopric. With Fulham Palace at his disposal, and as a refuge while out of favor with James

II, he set about expanding the gardens and building new conservatories. He then staffed his diocese, the Americas, with clergymen and missionaries whose secondary duty was to supply their bishop with exotic plants. As a result, Fulham soon contained the kingdom's largest single collection of New World specimens, including poison ivy.

THE PRINCELY SCIENCE

It is not excessive to say that New World plants were the rage of Europe at this time. If there was one problem with European botany after discovery of the New World, it was that there was no good way to handle the new arrivals. Until Columbus landed at Santo Domingo, Europe acknowledged only the roughly 600 plants that Dioscorides had cataloged in classical times—all presumed survivors, with Noah, of the flood. It is impossible today, therefore, to grasp the excitement and chaos that must have accompanied the new species that poured in for the first two centuries after Columbus. The continent was so awash in exotic specimens that science was overwhelmed. It took but one man, however, to calm the tumult.

At some point in the 17th Century a Swedish family had exchanged its old name, Ingemarsson, for that of a favored tree, the linden (*linné* in Swedish). As a result, their brightest son, Carl Linné (1707-1778), became known and revered in the English speaking world as Carl Linnaeus, not Ingemarsson.

Until 1753, when Linnaeus published his *Species Plantarum*, plants were identified casually by long, obscure Latin phrases (polynomials), often several conflicting ones. For example, John Tradescant had introduced poison ivy in the British Isles in 1632 as *Frutex canadensis epimedium folio*. In 1635 French botanist Jacques-Philippe Cornut (1606?-1651) classified it as *Hedera trifolia canadensis*, an ivy, in his *Canadensium Plantarum*. Cornut was never in the New World but based his studies on seeds and dried samples collected in Canada by Champlain and Cartier.

In the midst of the hubbub, a 17th-Century Swiss botanist, Gaspard Bauhin (1560-1624), was urging the wisdom of identifying each plant uniquely by no more than two words, essentially a given and family name. Bauhin used his system to list some 6,000 trees and plants, and the numbers kept increasing. By the beginning of the 18th Century a few botanists, like John Ray in England and Joseph de Tournefort in France, acknowledged the utility of Bauhin's idea. Yet even then plant names blossomed into polynomials.

Canadensium Plant. Historia. 97
EDERA TRIFOLIA CANADENSIS.

The first drawing of poison ivy, by Jacques Cornut

It was Linnaeus who fashioned a durable new system and got everyone else use it. To accomplish this he established 67 major orders of plants and published them in his *Philosophia Botanica* of 1751. Then, with characteristic energy and thoroughness, he gave every plant a single two-word Latin name, a binomial. It consisted of a one-word generic term (genus) and a one-word specific name (species). Each species was to have only one name, and everyone was to use it as long as it fit and was in the right genus. He then assigned every genus to one of his 67 orders. Strangely, Linnaeus gave no clue about what characteristics determined his orders. Since the majority contained inconsistent mixtures, many Linnaean genera were eventually abandoned.

Although theoretically plants are now classified by a single binomial, a number have conflicting names, each backed by its own party of advocates. Still, in the space of a very few years, the gifted Swedish botanist, teacher, encyclopedist, physician, and unabashed grandstander all but singlehandedly reorganized botany into its modern form. In recognition of the feat, he proclaimed himself the Prince of Botany. No one disputed his title.

In 1735, as a 28-year-old medical student in Sweden, Linnaeus had agreed to a three-year separation from his intended wife at her father's insistence and took his degree in Holland. After qualifying in his first week abroad, he soon won an appointment as physician and botanist to George Clifford, a wealthy Amsterdam banker. Then from the large gardens and library at Clifford's estate at Hartecamp he began to organize and publish his thoughts about classifying plants. From Holland he left to visit the major gardens in London and Oxford, and hugely impressed all he met.

Advancing on his own drive, charm, and easy persuasion of leading scientists that his system was the future, Linnaeus attracted a devoted and influential following. In his lifetime the scientific world, particularly in England and Holland, lionized him. Eventually appointed professor of botany at Uppsala University, he received a stream of books and plants for his garden, many of them sent by other naturalists who dreamed of immortality in a Linnaean genus. The Swedish crown gave him the honorific "von Linné." Of the pretty girl he married on his return from Holland, however, he confessed in time that he came to regard her "with fear and respect" for the remainder of his life.

Linnaeus reclassified poison ivy as *Rhus radicans*, instead of Cornut's proposal of *Hedera*, from a dried specimen, even though the plants were then available in England and possibly Europe. He might have saved modern botanists a lot of trouble if he had classified it from a live plant or retained the assistance of two naturalists then active in North America.

Mark Catesby (1683-1749), illustrator and author of *The Natural History of Carolina, Florida and the Bahama Islands*, was an admirer of Linnaeus but declined ever to adopt his or any other system. Members of Catesby's family established themselves early in Virginia, although Catesby returned to England after collecting his specimens. Among the professional hardships he faced was simply shipping samples to back England despite mildew, storms, pirates, and sailors who tippled rum from the specimen jars. In 1733 he was admitted to the Royal Society, and in 1741 showed the Society and reported on a poison ivy plant he had raised in a garden near Fulham. For at least a decade before that date, English nurserymen had been selling poison ivy plants to ordinary gardeners who presumably prized science above comfort. Oddly, by 1850 interest in poison ivy had so declined that the British medical journal *Lancet* reported a skin rash mysteriously confined to women and consequently called "hysterical dermatitis" until it turned out to afflict only housewives who tended the exotic vine on their cottages.

Catesby's plants and his book were two of the reasons why Linnaeus traveled to London and Oxford in autumn 1735. Just before this trip, John Clayton (1685-1773)—Clerk of the Court of Virginia and one of the few American members of the Royal Society—had sent Catesby his own large collection of seeds and dried plants. Clayton and Johann Friedrich Gronovius were co-authors of *Flora Virginica*, which with Catesby's was in the first rank of works on the plants of British North America. Catesby sent most of Clayton's specimens on to Gronovius in Holland for Linnaeus to study. Linnaeus observed the collections in England and Holland but made no use of a poison ivy specimen, dead or alive, from either. The opportunity was missed, and a later European visitor to North America joggled Linnaeus' aim in selecting the genus.

JÜNGSTROM LAUGHED

Far from being a visitor, Paul Dudley, commissioned Attorney General of Massachusetts Bay Colony in 1702, was born a third-generation American in Roxbury, Massachusetts, in 1675. He died there in 1751. Another American member of the Royal Society, he contributed several articles to its Philosophical Transactions, including a paper on the "Poyson-Wood Tree" or "Swamp Sumach." It already showed an un-English antipathy toward the species:

> It Never grows bigger than a Man's Leg, nor taller than an Alder, . . . ; as it is of quick growth, so it does not last long; the inside of the wood is yellow and very full of juice, as glutinous as Honey or Turpentine; and the Wood itself has a very strong unsavory Smell, but the Juice stinks

as bad as Carrion. Having thus described the Tree, we shall now proceed to give an account of its Poisonous Quality, &c.

1. And first, it must be observed that it poysons two ways, either by touching or handling of it, or by the Smell; for the Scent of it, when cut down in the Woods, or on the fire, has poisoned persons to a very great degree; One of my Neighbors was blind for above a Week together, with only handling it. And a Gentleman in the Country, sitting by his fire-side in the Winter, was swelled for several Days with the Smoak or flame of some Poyson-Wood that was in the fire.

2. A second thing to be remarked of the Poyson-Wood is, that it has this effect only on some particular Persons and Constitutions; for I have seen my own Brother not only handle, but chew it without any harm at all. And so by the same fire one shall be poysoned and another one not at all affected.

3. But then, Thirdly, this sort of Poyson is never Mortal, and will go off in a few Days of itself, like the Sting of a Bee; but generally the Person applies Plantain Water, or Sallet-Oyl and Cream.

4. As to its Operation, within a few Hours after the person is poysoned he feels an itching Pain that provokes a Scratching, which is followed by an Inflammation and Swelling; sometimes a Man's Legs have been poysoned, and have run with Water.

Dudley seems to be the earliest naturalist to note the species' idiosyncratic affliction of some people but not others, the virulence of smoke from the burning plant, and the notion that the oil was volatile and could poison at a distance. Every investigator after Dudley echoed the danger of noxious emanations, and it was nearly a century before that notion was dismissed scientifically if not in popular belief.

European governments by the middle 18th Century began to sense in the New World's novel and often nourishing plants the possibility of overcoming the continent's periodic famines. The Swedish government was the first to explore these resources by sending a botanist to search the Americas for food and forage suited to its climate. It chose for its agent a student of Linnaeus, Pehr, or Peter, Kalm (1716-1779). Also a physician and an accomplished botanist, Kalm was born in Åbo, Finland (then Sweden), and had accompanied Linnaeus on botanical trips to Russia and Ukraine in 1744. The Swedish Academy of Sciences charged Kalm with studying North American, particularly Canadian, plants for possible importation. Sailing from Gravesend, England, on August 5, 1748, with letters of introduction to Benjamin Franklin, the 28-year-old Kalm took with him as companion and servant, an expert gardener, Lars Jüngstrom. Jüngstrom may be the first recorded "I never get a rash" victim of the plants' venom.

During 1749, before leaving Pennsylvania for Canada, both Kalm and Jüngstrom had handled poison sumac and poison ivy with impunity to send samples to Sweden. Jüngstrom scoffed at warnings about it, he and Kalm having received accounts of eye-bungers, hoop snakes, soap-boilers, and other Pennsylvania whoppers. Both men, especially Jüngstrom, were dubious about tales of the juices of the poison tree. In any event, when they encountered it, it had no effect on either of them.

Their journey from Philadelphia to Québec in the following year occurred during a brief, unsettled lull in the French and Indian Wars called the Peace of Aix-la-Chapelle, which concluded King George's War or the War of the Austrian Succession, depending on which side of the Atlantic you were on. En route up the Hudson River by boat and on foot, Kalm and Jüngstrom with their guides passed through primeval woods forested with trees of an immensity unseen in Europe. Plagued by fears of rattlesnakes and unpacified Hurons, Kalm wrote of sleeping uneasily in the old forest, where they were awakened periodically by dreadful cracking noises as these rotting giants fell of their own age and weight.

In the winter of 1750, after their return from Canada, Kalm again warned Jüngstrom of the poisonous qualities of the "swamp sumach," but

Carl Linnaeus

. . . [Jüngstrom] only laughed, and looked upon the whole as a fable, in which opinion he was confirmed by his having often handled the tree the autumn before, cut many branches of it, which he had carried for a good while in his hand, in order to preserve its seeds, and put many into the herbals, and all this without feeling the least in- convenience. He would therefore, being a kind of philo- sopher, in his own way, take nothing for granted of which he had no sufficient proofs, especially as he had his own experience in the summer of 1749, to support the contrary opinion. But in the next summer his system of philosophy was overturned, for his hands swelled, and he felt a violent pain and itching in his eyes, as soon as he touched the tree, and this inconvenience not only attended him when he meddled with this kind of sumach, but even when he had any thing to do with the rhus radicans [poison ivy], or that species of sumach which climbs along the trees, and is not by far so poisonous as the former. By this adventure he was convinced of the power of the poison tree, that I could not easily persuade him to gather more seeds of it for me.

Kalm continues that he tried to catch the rash himself by spreading the oil upon his hands, cutting and breaking branches, peeling off the bark, rubbing his hands with it, smelling it, and carrying pieces of it in his bare hands, often and repeatedly without feeling the effects of the plant. At last he succeeded in these dubious efforts:

> On a hot day in summer, as I was in some degree of perspiration, I cut a branch of the tree, and carried it in my hand for about half an hour together, and smelt at it now and then. I felt no effects from it till in the evening; but next morning I awoke with a violent itching of my eyelids, and the parts thereabouts; and this was so painful, that I could hardly keep my hands from it. It ceased after I had washed my eyes for a while with very cold water; but my eye-lids were very stiff all that day; at night the itching returned; and in the morning as I awoke, it felt it as ill as the morning before, and I used the same remedy against it. . . . [I]t continued almost for a whole week together, and my eyes were very red, and my eye-lids were with difficulty moved during all that time. My pain ceased entirely afterwards. About the same time, I had spread the juice of the tree very thick upon my hand. Three days after they occasioned blisters, which soon went off without affecting much. I have not experienced any thing more of the effects of this plant, nor had I any desire so to do. However, I found that it could not exert its power upon me when I was not perspiring.

Kalm commented more kindly on poison ivy, which they also encountered:

> The rhus radicans is a shrub or tree which grows abundantly in this country, and has in common with the ivy, called hedera arborea, the quality of not growing without support either of a tree, a wall, or a hedge. I have seen it climbing to the very top of high trees in the woods, and its branches shoot out every where little roots, which

fasten upon the tree, and as it were enter into it. When the stem is cut, it emits a pale brown sap of a disagreeable scent. This sap is so sharp that the letters and characters made upon linen with it cannot be got out again, but grow blacker the more the cloth is washed. Boys commonly marked their names on their linen with this juice. If you write with it on paper the letters never go out, but grow blacker from time to time.

He and Jüngstrom assembled their collections to ship to England for forwarding to Sweden the following spring. Before his return in 1751 he married the widow of a pastor in Raccoon (now Swedesboro), New Jersey, whom he had met on his arrival and returned home with her. Linnaeus credited Kalm with discovery of 60 new species and named the American mountain laurel *Kalmia latifolia* after him, although it had been introduced earlier into Europe. One sample sheet Kalm gave Linnaeus contained the first known herbarium specimen of eastern poison oak. Also on the sheet was the three-leaved aromatic sumac, *Rhus aromatica*. Had the two plants not been displayed side by side, Linnaeus might have chosen a segregated genus rather than *Rhus* for poison ivy, oak, and sumac; and modern botanists would not have the difficulty they now have to advance *Toxicodendron* as the fitting genus for this ensemble.

THE DOUR SCOT

The fear of famine was also responsible, if indirectly, for identification of Pacific or western poison oak in the 19th Century. British interest in horticulture reached a peak at the end of the 18th and beginning of the 19th Century, stimulated by the specter of food shortages from a Malthusian population increase and a Napoleonic blockade. The Royal Horticultural Society was formed on June 29, 1801, to interest the landed gentry in better agricultural practices.

When improved husbandry and victories at the Nile and Trafalgar dispelled the threat of famine, the gentry, now prospering from their scientific advances, grew bored with the size of pig litters and demanded ornamental plants to brighten their country seats. Lacking what they considered sufficient native species for the task, they pressed the Society for exotic specimens suitable to the English climate. On the recommendation of a leading academic botanist, it sent David Douglas, one of the most remarkable botanical explorers in history, to satisfy his nation's demand for novelty.

Douglas was born on July 12, 1799, in Scone, Perthshire, Scotland. He died violently on July 13, 1834, at Kaluakauka, Hilo, Hawaii, when he fell or was pushed into a cattle pit-trap with a wild bull in it.

An unruly, difficult child with no early taste for learning, Douglas was apprenticed to a gardener at age 11. It unlocked his brilliance and a passion for horticulture. He advanced by hard study and work to the gardens at Valleyfield near Dunfermline, and had the good fortune to be trained by Sir William Jackson Hooker, professor of botany at Glasgow University. Hooker valued Douglas' enthusiasm and indefatigable assistance on plant collecting expeditions in the Scottish countryside. In the spring of 1823, in response to a letter from the Horticultural Society, Hooker recommended Douglas, then 24, to the Society for collecting specimens from the American Northwest.

In the following spring, after resolving institutional cross purposes, the Hudson's Bay Company agreed to receive the Society's botanical representative, and Douglas reached the mouth of the Columbia in early 1825.

Contemporaries describe Douglas as a short but energetic and powerful man, able to walk up to 50 miles a day if necessary, carrying his 60-pound pack of equipment and supplies. Once he packed 30 quires of paper—102 pounds—for collecting specimens. Others described him as stubborn, dour, humorless, and cantankerous. He was tireless to the end of his life. Of the many plants named after him, Douglas is remembered chiefly for the Douglas fir. The Douglas fir was first noted by Archibald Menzies in about 1792 as *Pseudotsuga taxifolia*. For a time, as *P. douglasii*, it commemorated the explorer who sent seeds of the commercially valuable tree to Great Britain. Only later was it reclassified *P. menziesii*, the binomial it now bears.

The British Columbia expedition of 1825 through 1827 was pure Douglas. He once forded a waist-high stream 14 times in one day while snowshoeing after specimens. He withstood a fever, which killed all the 450 inhabitants of three Indian villages and 24 Europeans, by taking his "healthful perambulations," those arduous botanical trips. He fought off a feverish chill by "sweating it out," then tramping 13 miles under full pack. Mice ate his seeds. Mold rotted his specimens. Pack rats carried off his razor and soap brush. He was swept 70 miles out to sea in a small boat that he and his companions had to bail out with their hats for two days before they could row back to safety. He suffered an infectious cut on his knee that laid him up for six months. And more than once his outings involved armed stand-offs with hostile tribesmen.

It is not surprising, therefore, that in 1830 on his last trip for the Society he dismissed as trifling the rash he got from packing the seeds of a Pacific poison oak shrub. He identified it as *Rhus lobata* and shipped his samples off to England.

A brooding man troubled by failing eyesight, Douglas inclined to judge himself harshly. He was not persuaded otherwise when discovering on a hero's return from his first expedition in 1827 that he was paid less than the Society's porter and that many of his specimens had been dumped in the corner of a storeroom to spoil. After a life of abstinence he began to drink and, while always reserved and reticent, began to have outbursts of garrulousness and irritability that may have contirbuted to his violent and mysterious death.

With Douglas' efforts, and those of Per Axel Rydberg in the 1890s, the entire North American poison ivy, oak, and sumac clan was present and accounted for. It only remained to get better acquainted.

3

"Touch it not!" exclaimed she, in a voice of
agony.
—*Nathaniel Hawthorne, "Rapaccini's Daughter"*

TOXICODENDRON PIE

HERE ARE TWO poison ivies, one in the eastern United States, one nearly everywhere; one is a bush, one a vine (but sometimes a bush). There are two poison oaks, one eastern, one western. There is one poison sumac, which inhabits the swamps and bogs of the eastern United States. Every state in the United States except Alaska, Hawaii, and Nevada is home to one or more of them, and poison ivy and oak are increasing their range because the American way of life suits them.

ANACARDIACEAE KITH AND KIN

None of the plants is an ivy or oak, although they once were classified with sumacs (*Rhus*). They belong to the Cashew Family, a worldwide group called Anacardiaceae after the heart-shaped (cardiac) fruit some of them bear. It is pronounced roughly "Anna-cardy-ACE-ee-yee." Heart-shaped here refers to the organ, not Valentine's Day. Most of the 600-odd species of Anacardiaceae worldwide are harmless, as are most of those native to North America. The family—Linnaeus' 21st Order—is divided into 76 genera, of which 25 (33 percent), are known to be injurious. Others may be.

Because poison ivies, oaks, and sumac have the family's noxious qualities, they were reclassified *Toxicodendron* (poisonous tree) in the 1930s and shifted away from *Rhus* to mingle with the genera whose most notable members are the cashew, the mango, and the oriental lacquer tree. Occasional reports still refer to poison ivy, oak, and sumac by the old Linnaean term, *Rhus*, although leading specialists prefer and use *Toxicodendron*. William T. Gillis, professor of botany at the University of Michigan, contends that, if in 1751 Peter Kalm had not given Linnaeus that specimen sheet which aromatic sumac (*Rhus aromatica*) shared with eastern poison oak, he may never have classified them *Rhus*. He also points out that Tournefort used a *Toxicodendron* generic as early as 1700. Joe Hennen, a botanist at Purdue University, found parasites that attack *Toxicodendron* species but not those of *Rhus*, while others do the reverse. Despite the botanists' pleas, articles and books still appear that muddle their way through the inadequate old *Rhus* classifications; and since the rash was medically classified before the name change, it appears in medical references as Rhus dermatitis.

Poison ivy, oak, and sumac's disagreeable properties mirror the rest of the family's. Cashew nuts and mangos—while nourishing and tasty—need special preparation, for, as plucked from the tree, they can cause the same rash as poison ivy, oak, and sumac with oils known as cardol, anacardol, and anacardic acid. Native to northern Brazil, cashews grow on a stem that swells into a safe, pear-shaped food, called a cashew apple. The cashew nut dangles below the apple inside a fruit which, with the nut, is rich in reactive oils. Roasting destroys the oils in cashew nuts, but workers who handle the fruit husks or stand in the smoke from roasting get frequent eye, skin, and lung irritations. Similarly, the mango's rind and the tree's leaves will cause a rash; and a mango blossom too zestfully sniffed can inflame the eyes and nose.

In Asia rashes were long an accepted occupational hazard for farmers and workers who handled the lacquer tree (*Toxicodendron vernicifluum*) and its varnish. Oriental lacquer, used in China as early as the 13th Century B.C., is the oldest known naturally occurring industrial plastic. Its resistance to bacterial attack, as well as to acids and alkalis, may be why the plant produces it. It is a phenolic resin that hardens by oxidization and polymerization. It takes heat up to 500 degrees fahrenheit, resists most solvents, insulates electrically as well as mica, and gives most people a rash. It is also extremely stable. Chinese lacquerware from 1,000-year-old tombs has caused rashes. A phenol, also called a "carbolic," is a mildly acidic compound first discovered in coal tar but also recoverable from other sources, including the sap of Anacardiaceae.

URUSHIOL, AND WELCOME TO IT

"Lacquer tree" is *tsuta urushi* in Japanese. So the Japanese research chemists who isolated and identified the oil named it *urushiol* (oo-ROO-she-ol) after the tree in a study they published in 1922. Soon afterward Charles R. Dawson, professor of chemistry at Columbia University, confirmed the oil's near identity to those in poison ivy, oak, and sumac. Earlier the oils had been called toxicodendrol, then lobinol. Urushiol—now a generic term for the gummy saps in the tiny subsurface duct glands of poison ivy, oak, and sumac—is nearly identical to the lacquer tree's and, like it, will give most people a rash. Also like the lacquer tree's it turns a hard, shiny black by polymerizing as it dries. Polymerization and oxidation deactivate the oil and render it less harmful. Water speeds oxidization. Since urushiol doesn't dissolve but darkens with successive washing, it was used briefly as a laundry marker, but with predictable side effects.

Although the oil of each plant differs slightly from the others, they all cross-sensitize, so that anybody allergic to one is allergic to all. They even cross-sensitize to the oil of raw cashews, cashew husks, mango rinds and leaves, the seed pulp of the ginkgo tree, and every other reactive species of Anacardiaceae. Urushiol in the stems, roots, leaves, flowers, and fruit of poison ivy, oak, and sumac stays in the plant year around. It can cause a reaction when the plants are dormant and for a long time after they are dead.

The persistent belief that extremely sensitive people can get a rash simply by being near the plant, while once supported by medical opinion, has been rejected scientifically since 1896 when Franz Pfaff (1850-1926), an American physician, distilled the sap and identified the residual oleoresin, not the vapors, as the irritant. Getting a rash requires touching the oil; and, because the plant's tiny oil ducts are under the surface, the plant must be bruised enough to release it. An animal's footstep or an insect's nibble is enough, especially with tender spring leaflets. Some writers suggest that "vaporous" allergies to the plants may be the result of either airborne ragweed pollen, which can cause its own rash, or vagrant insecticide sprays. Urushiol is, in fact, one of the least volatile of substances. It is more likely that the supposed victim of "airborne" urushiol inadvertently touched the plant or some object or pet that brushed against it, and either did not remember the contact or failed to connect the secondary contact to the plant. Still, as recently as 1986, a Pennsylvania State College Agricultural Sciences news release, either from a fit of urushiol madness or forgetful of Pfaff's efforts, warned of getting a rash when "the plant's oils are released into the air by the heat of a summer day. . . ."

Although poison ivy, oak, and sumac oils won't vaporize and cause a rash at a distance, they are tenacious compounds that won't dry up and go away, either. As noted, centuries-old herbarium samples have proven to be reactive. The author can confirm that a workshirt worn when he got a poison oak rash caused it again in the same spot after the shirt had been laundered—a fairly common experience. The oil will stick to pets, tools, clothing, shoes, steering wheels, golf clubs, firewood, or anything else for weeks or months to plague and torment the unlucky.

Urushiol is insoluble in water, resists drying, and stores very well. Poison-ivy leaves have been kept at room temperature for up to five years with no loss of virulence. Contaminated clothing has caused rashes even after more than one year. Poison ivy twigs immersed in water for sixteen months were still virulent, even though water gradually deactivates the oil by oxidization.

E.E. Bogue, an entomologist at the University of Ohio, reported in 1894 that he broke up poison ivy stems stored in a laboratory for at least three years, in order to put them in bottles to study borers that infested them. He got a rash between his fingers from the powdery, dry dust the borers had made in the stems.

Walter C. Muenscher and John M. Kingsbury of the Cornell University botany department cut a clump of poison ivy and spread it out on a garage roof to expose it to the weather for 18 months. At the end of that time it was as potent as ever. Roueché noted a well known experiment in which Muenscher and Kingsbury washed a white canvas glove, used 10 months earlier to collect poison ivy, in hot water and strong laundry soap for 10 minutes. They then dried and ironed it, and gave it to a volunteer to handle. Next day the volunteer developed a rash. Even burning does not vaporize or degrade urushiol, but lofts droplets of it into the atmosphere on particles of soot, by which it will cause head-to-toe dermatitis, lung irritation, uneasiness, fever, temporary blindness, and even death. Urushiol-laden smoke is the foremost hazard to forest-fire fighters, and the leading cause of injury on the fireline.

Urushiol is the fiercest allergen known. Pfaff determined that 1/1,000th of a milligram, a microgram, was enough to cause a rash. A gram is 0.0353 ounce. A whole ounce of urushiol can cause a rash in *28 million* people, and a drop the size of a pinhead can cause a rash in about 500. Sensitive people will get a rash from a skin patch with one-thousandth of one percent (0.001%) solution of urushiol on it. Researchers found by contrast that it takes a solution of 2.0 to 2.5 percent (2.0%-2.5%) of nickel to produce a rash on sensitized people's skin. People who are particularly sensitive to the oil may experience swelling of the eyes and throat, stomach cramps, nausea, vomiting, and diarrhea.

The only sure remedy, until effective controls are available, is to recognize and avoid the plants. That is not always easy, because, besides being inconspicuous and plentiful, they assume a bewildering array of forms. "Leaflets three . . ." is little help when the occasional leaf will bear up to 17 leaflets. Nor is leaf shape a consistent guide. Gillis identified dozens of subvarieties of poison ivy. All of the plants—poison ivies, oaks, and sumac—do, however, have common features that may help identify them. First, they never grow above 4,000 or 5,000 feet elevation. The leaves always grow up the stems alternately, rather than paired. When insect chewing releases the oil it may leave spots like black shiny beads on the leaves.

The whitish flowers yield tiny, pale, berry-like drupes (stone fruit, like cherries or peaches). These usually look white and waxy, although some may be fuzzy. Flowers and fruit always cluster on slender stems that grow from the angles between the leaves and woody twigs. They do not always flower and bear fruit. When the white or creamy clusters of fruit do occur they help identify the plants, especially after their leaves have fallen.

Even in their many guises, each individual species can be recognized and avoided through practiced observation. If it is not possible to spend time outdoors with someone who knows the live plants, a cautious walk through the woods with illustrations in hand is the best way to learn them. Try to see the plants at different seasons, looking at all their parts. It is all right to get close; just don't touch.

Vacationers should make an urushiol reconnaissance a first order of their stay. They will get no sympathy from the courts. Mrs. Kathryn Hersch rented a space from Anderson Acres trailer park in Ohio in the summer of 1939. When she got a poison ivy rash she sued, claiming that the park was negligent in not removing the weeds, in allowing them in the park, and in not destroying them. As a result of all that, she alleged, she sustained a severe case of dermatitis that incapacitated her for work and caused her to incur medical bills. A judge of the Ohio Appeals Court, after stating the legal principle for denying her claim, admonished that

> The city dweller who chooses to . . . vacation in the great outdoors must in addition to accepting fresh air and lake breezes assume the risks of the natural hazards of the outdoors such as flies, mosquitoes, snakes, poison ivy and other natural conditions not found in the urban communities.

POISON SUMAC

The botanical term for poison sumac is *Toxicodendron vernix*. *Vernix* means varnish. It is a rangy shrub or small tree with pale gray bark closely related to the lacquer tree (*T. vernicifluum*). It grows as a tall shrub or small tree, from five or six to 15 feet in height on average. In American Forests' *National register of big trees* for 1994, the largest confirmed specimen—in Chesapeake, Virginia—was 23 feet high. The plant's common names include poison tree, poison dogwood, poison elder, poison ash, swamp sumac, varnish sumac, and thunderwood. It is the only domestic *Toxicodendron*, or poisonous tree, that grows as a tree and it is the least varied of them.

Poison sumac (*Toxicodendron vernix*).

Its leaves, which resemble those of benign sumacs, have seven to 13 velvety leaflets 3" to 4" long and 1" to 2" wide. Unlike benign sumac leaves, the mid-rib from which the leaflets grow is usually, but not always, bright red. The leaves, dark green on top and light green beneath, are smooth edged, unlike respectable sumacs; they emerge bright orange in spring, turn dark green in summer, then yellow, orange, red, or russet in fall.

The range of poison sumac (*Toxicodendron vernix*).

Its abundant but small yellowish-green flowers rise from the angles of leaves along the smaller branches. They mature into ivory-white or green-colored fruits that hang loosely in clusters as long as 10 to 12 inches. Benign sumacs bear erect red fruits in a "stag-horn" fashion at the ends of their branches.

Commonest in the Great Lakes region, poison sumac grows from southern Québec to central Florida, predominantly east of the Mississippi, but sometimes in neighboring states west of the river. It likes bogs, swamps, and wet bottom lands, where good sumacs never go. The occasional plant, usually from seed excreted by a bird, will sprout in dry soil, short and spindly, but still able to afflict those who encounter it outside its native haunts.

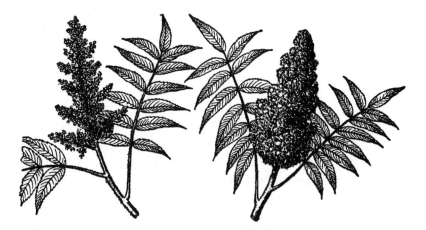

Staghorn sumac (*Rhus typhina*) has leaves with "toothed" margins and bears upright terminal flowers and fruit in a "staghorn" display.

CLIMBING POISON IVY

Common or climbing poison ivy is *Toxicodendron radicans*. *Radicans* means rooting. It is also called poison vine, markweed, three-leaved ivy, Gowitch, picry, climbing sumac, (erroneously poison oak), and poison creeper among others.

It is usually a vigorous, rope-like hairy vine that can also grow as a creeper, as a medium shrub, or a small one in shady forested spots. Very long lived, its vines can grow 75 feet long and 6 or 7 inches thick. The hairs on the vines are aerial roots that look like reddish fuzz on new growth but coarsen and darken as the plant matures. An old vine covered with these hairs may look like a fuzzy rope. The hairs have an adhesive that binds the vine to whatever it climbs on. It sends out roots where it contacts the ground or anything that will support it. It doesn't spiral but grows straight up its host, favoring the grooves in rough bark. While not parasitic, it may smother or starve the host plant. All its parts—leaves, stems, fruit, and roots—cause a rash.

In some parts of the country, when in full sun, it grows as a low-growing shrub 6" to 30" tall. One specimen on Sanibel Island, Florida, was recorded to be a tree standing 15 to 20 feet high. In either form it has an extensive root system that grows just below ground level. The leaves usually have three leaflets. The middle leaflet is larger on a longer stem than the lateral or side leaflets. As noted, some plants have been found with up to 17 leaflets per leaf.

The great variation in the shape or lobing of the leaflets almost defies description. On

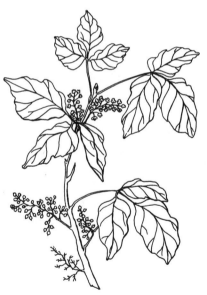

Climbing poison ivy (*Toxicodendron radicans*).

the East Coast it has smooth-margined leaves, but one variation in the central states has notches or teeth on its leaves. Another variety, *verrucosum*, from Oklahoma's Arbuckle mountains through the Edwards plateau of Texas, has a deep, sharp lobe on either side of the central leaf and on the outside edge of each side leaf. The Rio Grande basin variety, *eximium*, may have round-lobed leaves that resemble the club in a deck of cards. To make matters worse, with increasing disturbance of natural sites, the subspecies have started migrating and hybridizing. In some forms, the fruit is covered with fine hair, giving it a downy appearance. Usually, however, it is entirely smooth. All poison ivy varieties become dormant and leafless in winter; so the fruit helps to identify them from late fall through early spring.

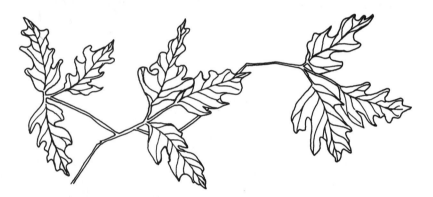

The deeply lobed verrucosum subvariety of T. radicans.

Poison ivy follows civilization, cropping up in disturbed sites like cut banks, lake shores, roadsides, old fence rows, utility poles, railroad embankments, playgrounds, vacant lots, back yards, and around buildings. Look for it around fence posts, trees, poles, and other convenient roosts for birds, its usual means of transportation. It prefers woodland borders and clearings, and shuns dense forest. Except for occasional brilliant fall color, it is unobtrusive and blends in with harmless climbers like Virginia Creeper and Boston ivy, which, with other domestic vines, it slightly resembles. More than one unsuspecting householder has trained it up a trellis or wall.

The eximium variety of *T. radicans*, with leaves somewhat suggesting clubs in a deck of cards.

RYDBERG POISON IVY

The other poison ivy, named *Toxicodendron rydbergii*, after its discoverer Per Axel Rydberg (1860-1931), lacks aerial roots and is a bushy variant of *radicans*. It is called Rydberg poison ivy or occasionally Canadian poison ivy, and is the most widespread and uniform variety. Swedish-born Rydberg, once curator of the New York Botanical Garden, was educated at the University of Nebraska and Columbia University. A botanical field agent for the U.S. Department of Agriculture in the summers of 1891 through 1896, his description of the species appeared in a later monograph on the Anacardiaceae. Linnaeus knew of this species but grouped it with *radicans*. Besides lacking root hairs, *rydbergii* has larger fruit and leafstalks, with broader leaflets folded in a spoon shape. The extensive root systems of both *rydbergii* and *radicans* sometimes spread 20 feet, just under the surface, and provide excellent erosion control.

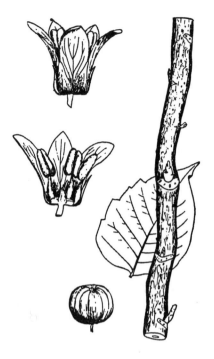

Leaf, stem, flowers, and fruit of *T. rydbergii*. No root hairs.

Rydbergii seeks flood plains, bottom lands, lake shores, and dunes. It is nearly absent from the poor soil of scrubby oak and pine savannahs of the Southeast, and from oak and hickory woods. It likes the same habitats as willows but never grows with them. It grows nearly everywhere in the United States east of the Cascade mountains, and north and east of Nevada. The *rydbergii* form is the only variety north of the 44th parallel of latitude and west of meridian 101, excepting eastern Arizona and Texas. It is everywhere in Mexico except the Yucatan and northern Baja California. Its southern limit is the Huehuetenango Department of Guatemala. Its northern limit is an irregular line from the Gaspé peninsula of Québec to British Columbia, along the 52nd parallel.

Both poison ivies produce inconspicuous flowers in clusters that rise on the side of the stem just above a leaf. Often the flowers do not develop or they produce no fruit. *Rydbergii*'s tiny fruit is white and waxy with pumpkin-like ripples on the outer surface. Usually it is entirely smooth, but sometimes, like variants of *radicans*, it is covered with fine hair and looks downy.

The poison ivies are the most widespread *Toxicodendron* species in the United States and are also found in Bermuda, the Bahamas, Taiwan, Japan, western and central China, and as far south as Malaysia. The fossil record shows that poison ivy originated in North America about 80 million years ago and migrated to Asia over what are now the Bering Straits. It did not find its way to Europe, one of whose surprised early visitors here, Captain John Smith, named it poison ivy for us.

The combined range of *T. radicans* and *T. rydbergii*.

EASTERN POISON OAK

Eastern poison oak—*Toxicodendron toxicarium* (poison bearing) or *T. quercifolium* (oak-leaved) or *T. pubescens* (fuzzy)—bears three competing names, although experts favor *toxicarium*, the earliest. Because Linnaeus had classified it *Rhus toxicodendron*, it might have fallen into a tautonymic limbo without the benefit of at least one species name to fit its new genus.

It is only distantly related to poison ivy and differs from it significantly. They rarely hybridize, yet it is often confused with poison ivy shrubs and called oakleaf poison ivy, for no very good reason. Its three leaflets look velvety. The lighter color on the underside of the leaves is caused by fine surface hairs. Stems generally grow upright. The shrubs have slender branches, often also covered with fine hairs that give the

The range of *T. toxicarium, quercifolium* or *pubescens*.

whole plant a downy look. Its leaves have three leaflets that are lobed, a little like the leaves of eastern white oaks (*Quercus alba*). The middle leaflet usually is lobed alike on both edges and resembles a small oak leaf, but the two side leaflets often have lopsided lobing. This one does inhabit the scrub oak savannahs and pine barrens of Atlantic and Gulf coastal plains, living in those poor sandy soils and sand-hill forests that poison ivy usually avoids. Its range overlaps poison ivy's but the two seldom grow together because of their different physical needs.

It never climbs or produces aerial roots. Its fruits are fuzzy like the rest of the plant, and they are more heart-shaped and larger than those of poison ivy in the same range. Its form varies less, although male plants have more deeply lobed leaves.

Centered mainly in the southeastern United States, it ranges from southern New Jersey to Marion County Florida, west to eastern Texas and Cherokee County, Kansas, where it grows beyond the range of the pine and scrub oak forests, typically with a bunchgrass understory. That extends it into Oklahoma, western Arkansas, and Missouri.

WESTERN OR PACIFIC POISON OAK

Western or Pacific poison oak, *Toxicodendron diversilobum* (variously lobed), is closely related to poison ivy and interbreeds with *rydbergii* in the Columbia River Gorge. Hybrids there are spreading out in both directions to further confuse plant recognition. Although David Douglas ignored his slight rash when he sent the seeds to Great Britain from Vancouver Island, he did urge locating the plants well off the garden path.

This species ranges from southern British Columbia to northern Baja California, squeezed between the coast and the Cascades, Sierra Nevadas, and Mojave desert, up to an elevation of 5,000 feet. It is also called oakleaf ivy and yeara, after the Spanish explorers' *yiedra* (ivy) and *yiedra maligna*.

Like poison ivy, it has three leaflets and grows as a vine or shrub, but it has larger leaves than poison ivy and its autumn color is a deeper red. Its variable leaflets, which may resemble leaves of a Coast live oak (*Quercus agrifolia*), Valley oak (*Q. lobata*), or neither, justify its specific—*diversilobum*. They may be lobed deeply, shallowly, or not at all, symmetrically or asymmetrically, and with a flat, curled, or crumpled surface. They are leathery and dark in full sun or delicate, thin, and light green in shade. There also is enough regional variation from north to south to compound the confusion. In spring the leaves are pale green, but sometimes red. They turn yellow-green in summer and make the Pacific Coast's best fall colors, orange-scarlet to brilliant magenta, giving them entree to the occasional fall bouquet. Three leaflets are the norm but sometimes also it has five, seven, or up to 17 leaflets per leaf, often on the same plant. Leaves seldom are longer than 6 or 7 inches or wider than the palm of the hand. Usually they are the size of a quarter—or a half dollar, if you remember half dollars.

Its flowers grow in clusters on slender stems from the angle of the leaf. Individual flowers are greenish white and about ¼ inch across. The flower clusters mature around mid-October into greenish or creamy flattened berries, about the size of small currants. Many plants do not fruit; others bear heavily.

Typically this poison oak grows three to five feet high, mostly as a rank upright shrub with lots of small woody stems. Older branches are gray and become elbowed, cracked, and gnarled. Sap from injuries dries black. While its stems are not hairy like poison ivy, it can develop adventitious aerial roots and climb like poison ivy. Although these roots attach it to things, its branches grow upright and don't depend entirely on other objects for support. In some woodland areas of California, 70 to 80 percent of the trees support 25- to 30-foot high vines. Lacking trees, it will settle for utility poles and fence

Western or Pacific poison oak (*Toxicodendron diversilobum*).

posts. Its roots spread out vigorously and send up new shoots. Once sprouted, it will take over. It can spread sideways to make a thicket, or lie low where it is windblown or grazed by deer.

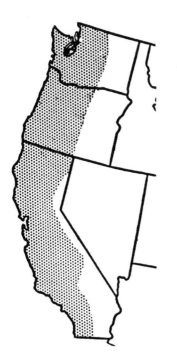

The range of T. diversilobum.

In open pastures it usually grows in spreading clumps, crowds out grazing land, and threatens most people who work in such areas or tend cattle that touch the plants while grazing. It has no effect on cattle or other browsing animals, although dogs and cats occasionally have eye infections from nosing around in it. Agricultural studies show that it is a good browse plant, reasonably high in protein. Horses prefer it to other woody shrubs; sheep, goats, and deer browse on it a little less, and cattle still less.

It was formerly less common but, like others of its kind, it has moved into disturbed sites. It is now the most widely distributed wild shrub in California, expanding its turf in the tracks of deforestation and other human endeavors. It appears along cut banks, rights-of-way, roadsides, floodplains, river terraces, on roadside fences, and in empty lots and playgrounds. It is nowhere happier than on a picnic ground. It seeks cool spots like north facing banks and the shelter of real oaks. It likes mild winters, filtered shade, and ready moisture but dry feet. It may be the vigorous understory in seasonal creek beds where its long whip-like stems are a hiker's nightmare. A final, insidious source of trouble is the black lacquer from its quickly polymerizing sap, which in summertime can speckle leaves and trees in windy areas or along busy, dusty roads.

Unlike daffodils, oleander, foxglove, or nightshade, none of these plants are poisonous, any more than they are true ivies or oaks, or ordinary sumacs. No one knows why they afflict only humans, other primates, and the odd guinea pig or laboratory mouse. But they do. Unsporting as that may seem, a look at the human allergic response will at least explain what causes the rash and where the best chance for relief lies.

4

"How do you account for it Ridgeon? Have we over-stimulated the phagocytes? . . . Nay, have they finally begun to prey on the lungs themselves? Or on one another? I shall write a paper about this case. . . . "

—George Bernard Shaw, THE DOCTOR'S DILEMMA

URUSHIOL DERMATITIS

ERHAPS the crowning paradox of poison ivy, oak, and sumac is exactly why they cause a rash. For just as poison oak and ivy are neither ivies nor oaks, there is not a drop of poison in them or in poison sumac. Urushiol, which causes the problem, is neither poisonous nor—except in unnaturally high concentrations—irritating. The rash is an allergy attack, a contact *dermatitis* (skin inflammation) that afflicts only people who have developed an *immune response* to an otherwise harmless oil. People who are not "immune" do not react; and, unless they get the requisite defenses, they will not react.

Like all allergy attacks, urushiol dermatitis results from the immune system's attacking a foreign but innocent intruder. Almost as if to certify the material's innocence, the system needs to "learn" it before it can respond. Thus, except for the "exquisitely" sensitive, a first brush

47

with urushiol seems uneventful, because all it normally does is give the system a chance to weigh the potential threat. Even then, if it finds one, it still needs five or six more days to fashion its defense. In those few days the average person can re-contact the substance freely with no risk of harm whatever. If, after those first few days, the plants disappear from one's life forever, so will the chance of a rash.

Because first encounters with urushiol usually pass without notice, chances are there will be a later contact. And once past the five- or six-day grace period most people will get a rash the next time around, even from a small amount of the oil and even if years go by. Some are fooled by needing repeated exposures to become sensitive—or to lose their *in*sensitivity. These are the victims who "never get a rash." But once sensitized, by one or many exposures, the next contact will provoke a rash which will return with greater severity at each later contact. Usually, the longer the time between exposures, the less violent is the reaction. That is only a norm. While sensitivity increases for most people through repeated exposures, it may decrease for others. Unconfirmed reports state that lacquer and cashew workers gradually build a resistance to their respective products. It may also be that the only ones who stay on the job are those who eventually resist or tolerate the oils. Sensitivity also slowly varies over time; it is seldom the same from year to year.

SOME ESSENTIALS OF ALLERGY

Allergies have been called immunological mistakes. They are violent aberrations of a system intended to attack and repel *pathogens* ("disease makers") and maintain good health. Pathogens, along with the debris of minor incidents like scratches and insect bites, belong to a larger population called *antigens*. Antigen means, roughly, a "trouble maker," and except for real pathogens an antigen should not be, and usually is not, a major immunological event.

The body's first bulwark against antigens is an unbroken, hostile skin surface. The skin is covered by corrosive lactic and fatty acids, which dull razor blades, turn cheap jewelry green, and try to dissolve vagrant antigens. It is also crowded with resident microorganisms called *normal flora* that don't want new neighbors and do all they can to discourage them. Tears and other fluids seeping from body orifices engulf and wash out most antigens that try to enter that way; but they can still get in with swallowing, inhalation, sexual contact, and from mother to child.

If antigens breach or infiltrate these first barriers, the immune system rallies to the defense, signaling its mobilization with familiar alarms. The standard accompaniment is inflammation around the breach—an angry red, hot, and swollen spot. Extra blood flows to the site and reddens the skin. The skin swells when local blood vessels expand and leak blood plasma (fluid) with anti-antigen proteins. The swelling causes some of the pain, but the immune system also releases enzymes to irritate the nerve endings. Other enzymes generate heat to speed up the process. There are even special proteins, *lymphokines*, one of whose tasks is to create that familiar under-the-weather feeling that goes with illness.

Antigens are invariably microorganisms of one sort or another. Microorganisms—loosely "germs"—include viruses, bacteria, fungi, protozoa (microscopic animals), and sometimes helminths (nematodes or roundworms). Of the millions of microorganisms we wade through every day, however, only a few are antigens. Fewer are pathogens. Most are harmless. Some, like those in the intestines that turn food into usable substances, are essential for survival.

In addition to antigens, there is a seemingly innocuous class that may arouse, not just a response, but a surprising fury of decontamination. The immune system, sensing in this class more than a passing likeness to antigens, may even exceed certain biological limits to seek and destroy them. One such limit is size or mass. For the immune system to recognize and attack it, an antigen needs a molecular weight heavier than 10,000 daltons. Smaller than that and the immune system should ignore it. A dalton is very small, 1/12 the mass of a carbon-12 atom.

Allergens, the substances that cause an allergy attack, are often much less than 10,000 daltons and ought to slip quietly past our immune defenses. There is a significant exception to the rule, however, where dermatitis is concerned. That exception is the *hapten*, a non-protein molecule, usually smaller than 1,000 daltons, but with an affinity for bonding with protein molecules. When haptens bond with body tissue cells they form a *neoantigen*, say, a close-enough trouble maker. They

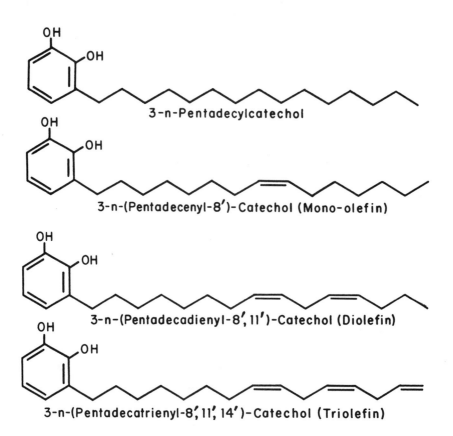

OH
OH
3-n-Pentadecylcatechol

OH
OH
3-n-(Pentadecenyl-8')-Catechol (Mono-olefin)

OH
OH
3-n-(Pentadecadienyl-8',11')-Catechol (Diolefin)

OH
OH
3-n-(Pentadecatrienyl-8',11',14')-Catechol (Triolefin)

Poison ivy catechols.

are close enough to suit the average immune system and excite a response.

The allergens that cause urushiol dermatitis are light, nontoxic molecules that act as haptens. The drawings of poison ivy and oak catechols illustrate the long, unstable side chains that appear to give these oils their sticky quality. The compounds vary from plant to plant and within different parts of the same plant. Poison ivy's allergic principle is slightly different from poison oak's. That doesn't matter. All the catechols cross-sensitize their victims.

Researchers believe that, once inside the skin, the catechols first oxidize into a more reactive form called *quinones*. The quinones in turn bond with the skin proteins. Even though the bonding molecules may be harmless (like urushiol) or beneficial (like penicillin), the immune sys-

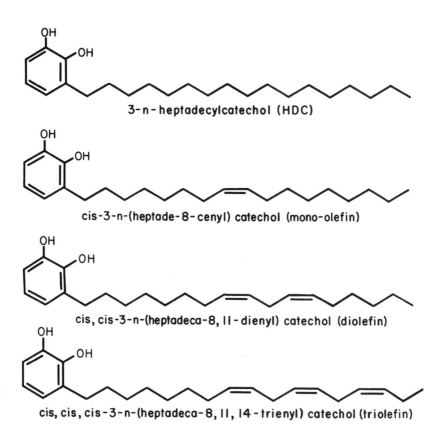

3-n-heptadecylcatechol (HDC)

cis-3-n-(heptade-8-cenyl) catechol (mono-olefin)

cis, cis-3-n-(heptadeca-8, II-dienyl) catechol (diolefin)

cis, cis, cis-3-n-(heptadeca-8, II, I4-trienyl) catechol (triolefin)

Western poison oak catechols.

tem perceives the combination of these molecules and our skin cells as deviant or cancerous. Once embarked on its cleansing mission, the immune system, potent enough to defeat the deadliest diseases, will lay waste not only to the intruders but to participating body tissues, as well.

THE LYMPHATIC LINE-UP

The immune response is extremely complex and far from fully understood. Any explanation for non-specialists must be oversimplified and will be soon out of date. What follows is hugely abbreviated and generalized but may suggest why folk remedies don't work the way some people think they do and why some proposed medical controls probably will work.

Two kinds of white blood cells (*leukocytes*) predominate in the immune response. Both leave the bone marrow as immature *stem cells* and become T cells or B cells. B cells are named after the Bursar of Fabricius in birds where they first observed, and T cells (generally grouped into T4's and T8's) are named after the thymus gland just over the heart, to which some stem cells migrate from the bone marrow.

A special hormone in the thymus turns the stem cells into T cells, and sends them to wait in the spleen and lymph nodes. B cells go directly from the bone marrow to the spleen and lymph nodes. The lymphatic system is a network of vessels that mirrors the circulatory system and bathes our tissues in a beneficial, clear fluid. The lymph nodes are enlarged stations in the system where leukocytes shuttle between the lymphatic and circulatory systems.

B cells, a mainstay of immunity, produce *antibodies*, each of which is specially tailored to combat every individual antigen that invades the body. Scientists estimate that the human body has about one million different B cells, which can produce over one million antibodies. To build new antibodies, B cells get the assistance of special T4 cells, fittingly called *helpers*. T helpers normally turn on the immune response and help B cells change into *plasma* cells. The plasma cells, still coached by helpers, then fashion the antigen-specific antibodies. Because many antibodies remain for life to protect against the same antigen, should it ever reappear, immunologists and immunobiologists develop vaccines, often of weakened antigens or their derivatives. These serums cause the production of antibodies against just such potential full-strength invaders.

B cells' antibodies are called *immunoglobulins*, abbreviated to *Ig*. Specifically, they are *immunoglobulin G*, or *IgG*, cells, sometimes called "B memory cells." Of the body's five immunoglobulins, IgG's predominate, normally making up about 80 percent of the total.

To overcome an antigen, the B cells' new custom-built antibodies stick to them, forming an antigen-antibody complex that neutralizes the antigen. During the response a slurry of immune-system proteins creates an environment hostile to antigens and assists a complex attack, by other immune components that include:

Phagocytes, white cells whose name literally means cell-eaters, although they simply engulf the antigens while other components degrade them;

Macrophages, literally big eaters, more highly developed phagocytes that serve several functions, including presenting antigens for T helpers to identify; and

Granulocytes, leukocytes that carry granules of chemicals in their cell fluid for degrading antigens. There are four kinds of granulocytes. Two of them, basophils and mast cells, eventually participate to a very minor degree in the urushiol dermatitis response.

The other T cell (T8) comes in two major groupings, *suppressors* and *cell-killers*. Just as the helpers turned on the immune response, the suppressor turns it off when the other immune components have finished the job. Weeks, occasionally months, or even years may pass before the suppressors end a response. There are other T cells to keep the suppressors from ending the response too soon.

Every cell, whether an antigen's or the body's, bears an identifying molecular code on its surface. Every T8 or T4 cell has "receptor molecules" on its surface that lets it read these codes and recognize "nonself" cells when they enter the body. In an urushiol dermatitis response, it is the T killer cells—not the T helpers—that spot the urushiol haptens and begin the response. This influences how the immune system responds.

INSIDE URUSHIOL DERMATITIS

No B cells or immunoglobulins are involved in urushiol dermatitis. What floods the skin at first are phagocytes, macrophages, and T cells along with the *lymphokines* they release. Lymphokines are proteins that act on and direct the T cells, phagocytes, macrophages, and body cells to respond to antigens or neoantigens.

Lymphokines are centrally important to a dermatitis attack. Using a biological signal-and-delivery system called *chemotaxis*, they direct immune components and the body during the reaction. One variety attracts macrophages to the site. Other lymphokines keep them from wandering away, and others urge them on to increased activity against the allergen. Lymphokines from T-helper cells urge young T cells in the lymph nodes to mature fast into T-killer cells specifically for attacking the foreign substance.

An urushiol dermatitis reaction has three phases. During the first 24 hours, while the above is taking place, the skin becomes itchy, red, and swollen. In the second phase, about 48 hours into the attack, T cells—primarily cell killers—which have been mediating the response, cause local blood vessels to increase in size and porosity, letting plasma and lymphocytes seep into the tissues. Blisters begin to appear and coalesce.

In the final phase, some 72 hours along, swelling, pain, and blisters worsen. The blisters burst. Weeping begins. It takes about four more days for this final phase to subside. The mast cells and basophils activated during the attack's second and third phases appear to release too few histamines or other mediators to affect on the reaction; so antihistamines do little more than make the victim drowsy.

OOZE, RUPTURE, AND CRUST

T-killer cells destroy by *cytolysis* ("site-ALL-iss-iss"), cell-disintegration. They release chemicals that perforate cell walls and let the contents ooze out. Leaking cell fluid mingles with all the plasma and lymphatic fluids of the response. The result is inflammation, itching, blistering, skin-tissue breakdown, and ooze. That ooze is another source of misunderstanding.

Allergies are not contagious. The urushiol in each cell is either so highly diluted or tightly bonded to the cell fragments that the fluid seeping from the blisters won't spread the rash. American physician Thomas Horsfield (1773-1859), who spent many years as a botanist studying the plant life of the East Indies and later maintained the East India Company Museum in London, reported in his dissertation of 1798 that he tried several times to spread the rash by inoculating healthy skin with fluid from the blisters but could not "excite the infection."

Horsfield's was the first immunological study of poison ivy dermatitis. His experiment, usually uncredited, was often repeated with the same result. A very short list of the replications includes those by: J.

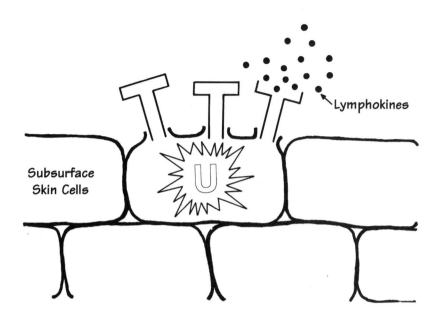

Prepared urushiol-specific T cells (T8s) identify skin cells with urushiol haptens as non-self (deviant) and attack them, releasing lymphokines.

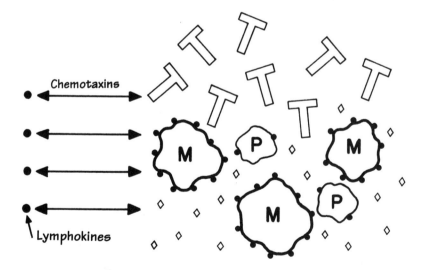

Chemotaxins from the lymphokines attract more T cells, phagocytes, macrophages, and the migration inhibition factor (those diamonds).

Bigelow, 1817; S.C. Busey, 1873; J.C. White, 1873; E. von Adelung, 1913; E.D. Brown, 1922; G.L. Krause and F.D. Weidman, 1925; M.B. Sulzberger and J.H. Katz, 1943. Each researcher reached Horsfield's conclusion: the fluid did not spread the rash. By contrast, the fluids from ruptured cells infected with a *virus* contain live, potent viruses like smallpox, chicken pox, shingles, and herpes. Those fluids will spread the disease and any itch that goes with it. Dermatitis ooze, unlike the viral kind, is nearly pure body fluid—wet but harmless. Scratching the rash can cause secondary infection, however, which will prolong and worsen the condition. Also, as long as the oil is on the skin, scratching may spread it around and cause later outbreaks.

After the reaction runs its course and T suppressor cells end it, a few thousand of the custom-made T killer cells stay on as T "memory" cells like their IgG counterparts. When urushiol next bonds with skin proteins they will mobilize to cause another rash.

After the dermatitis attack, urushiol-specific T-memory cells remain to start a response on the next contact with the oil.

DELAYED HYPERSENSITIVITY

Allergic dermatitis takes two forms. One, an *immediate hypersensitivity reaction*, is more common and usually is not very serious. A few who are extremely sensitive, however, can experience a potentially lethal anaphylactic shock from such a reaction. The more widely troubling form—including poison ivy, oak, or sumac rashes—is technically a *Type IV Delayed Hypersensitivity Reaction.*

Immediate hypersensitivity reactions like those from insect bites cause the skin to get hot, red, and to swell softly within a few seconds or minutes of the bite. For most of us the skin returns to normal after a few minutes, or hours at worst. The reaction in a delayed hypersensitivity attack can take 24 to 72 hours to appear. The affected skin also becomes red and warm, but the swelling is firm. The reaction will last for days and will kill part of the tissue involved. Tuberculosis, a chronic infectious disease not an allergy, causes a similar hypersensitivity response that gradually destroys lung tissues over a period of years. It usually kills its victim if antibiotics don't get the bacterium first. The leprosy bacterium causes a similar tissue attack, as do the fungus in athlete's foot and certain yeast and mold infections.

Research into tuberculosis helped suggest why the Type IV hypersensitivity reaction is delayed. The delay is called the Koch Phenomenon and is explained by an experiment in 1882 by Dr. Robert Koch. He injected a group of guinea pigs with tuberculosis bacteria. In 10 days to two weeks the illness spread throughout their bodies, and they died soon after. Later, he injected another group of guinea pigs with the bacteria, and some days later injected them again. Antigens from the second injection, however, did not spread. Instead the immune system walled them off, caused a hypersensitivity reaction at the injection site, and killed the infection. (The guinea pigs died from the first shot, anyway).

Koch's experiments led to the tuberculosis patch test. People who have not been exposed to TB get no skin response from the weak TB derivative on the test patch. Those who have been exposed, and whose systems recognize the bacterium or its derivatives, get the same walled-off itchy and reddened area around the patch after one or two days that Dr. Koch's animals got from the second shot. Modern researchers concluded from Koch's observations that, on average, it took 12 to 24 hours for T-memory cells from the earlier dose to collect and train enough new T cells to wall off the infection. It took another 12 to 24 hours to muster enough lymphokines to inflame the area. Combined, both processes occur over 24 to 48 hours, about the time it takes an urushiol dermatitis response to start. This is another average, of course, and reaction time can vary from four hours to 10 days.

THANKS FOR THE IMMUNITY

Medical essayist Lewis Thomas, M.D., suggested that our body's response to many antigens is at times so massive that *it* is what sickens and kills us. While his may be a minority view where pathogens are concerned, it has a compelling logic for allergic responses. Most allergens, including urushiol, are intrinsically harmless. Yet the response to inhalation of urushiol-laden smoke can cause death by suffocation from tracheitis. It is just as effective as TB but faster.

For a lucky few—about 15 to 25 percent—the immune system will always treat the urushiol hapten as the harmless stuff it is. These few will never get a rash. For the rest, our immune system, which is there to overcome the threat of pathogens, occasionally throws a self-destructive fit when a harmless substance bonds with skin proteins. There is a glimmer of hope, however, because the human body constantly changes. Its allergic responses evolve and may vanish voluntarily and entirely. The author has met two people who worked outdoors and suffered from repeated on-the-job encounters with urushiol. Eventually, it stopped giving them rashes. They may have been in the minority who develop a resistance to it. It is just as likely that, as their immune systems weakened with age, their hypersensitivity reactions receded and disappeared. Once gone, an allergy rarely returns. While an allergic debility may not be lifelong, its decline is cold comfort if it only reflects the immune system's slow collapse. The remedy everyone has been looking for is a limited and quicker collapse, but only for one allergen.

5

Fillet of a fenny snake,
In the cauldron boil and bake;
Eye of newt, and toe of frog,
Wool of bat, and tongue of dog . . .
–William Shakespeare, MACBETH, Act IV, Scene 1

PALLIATIVES & PREVENTIVES

IKE ALL ALLERGIES, urushiol dermatitis can be treated but not cured. Folk efforts to overcome it have flourished since long before the arrival of the first colonists, whose resort to plantain juice or salad oil Paul Dudley noted in the 18th Century. In recent decades medicine has advanced significantly on it, and complete control, so far elusive, may soon be within its reach. If it is not, the search will continue, as urushiol dermatitis and occasional systemic poisoning are costly and potentially lethal disorders.

It is particularly hazardous to forestry, utility, and agricultural workers. United States Forest Service informants said that it accounts for at least 10 percent of the service's lost time injuries. The percentage is much higher in bad fire years. Exposure to smoke on the fire-line has caused dermatitis over the entire body, respiratory tract inflammation, fever, temporary blindness, and even death from throats swollen shut.

In 1991 poison oak rashes made up 21.7 percent of workers' compensation dermatitis claims in California. That was 0.18 percent of total claims. They represent only the reported cases. Nobody knows how many people get urushiol dermatitis each year. Physicians need not report urushiol dermatitis cases, and no one has surveyed a sample and applied the results to the population at large. Doctor Epstein recently estimated between 40 and 60 million cases each year. Inquiries to the National Institutes of Health, the National Center for Health Statistics, the National Arthritis and Musculoskeletal and Skin Diseases Information Center, the Asthma and Allergy Foundation, the Institute of Allergy and Infectious Diseases, and Vincent Beltrani, M.D., of the Contact Dermatitis Committee of the American Academy of Allergy and Immunology produced no firm figures. For most purposes it is enough to say that a lot of us will get a rash this year.

Although it is an allergy, urushiol dermatitis differs from other allergies in several major respects. First, as much as 85 percent of the population are potentially susceptible to it; 50 percent are clinically allergic, that is, likely to get it directly from the plants. By contrast, no more than 20 percent of the population have the standard allergies (hay fever, asthma, eczema, and hives, as well as sinusitis and sensitivities to cat dander, dust mites, and the like). Second, urushiol dermatitis victims typically are not allergic to anything else. Textbook allergics commonly have more than one standard allergy (which may result in some double counting). Yet nearly half of all allergics, particularly eczema patients, are entirely resistant to urushiol dermatitis, apparently because their higher production of B antibodies somehow interferes with the T-cells' response. Third, although some researchers suggest a hereditary resistance to urushiol, as with most allergies, parents who are insensitive to it may have sensitive offspring.

BEAT THE ITCH

The invariable response to a knowing brush with urushiol is to try to get it off before it gets in. Complete removal requires uncommon alacrity. Some reports advise that within 10 to 20 minutes of contact, urushiol molecules penetrate the skin surface and bond with inner skin cells. Others suggest a three-minute bonding time, which seems nearer the mark. In an experiment on nine volunteers in 1943, Dallas clinician J.B. Howell showed that washing with strong laundry soap one minute after contact prevented a reaction in five slightly to moderately sensitive people but was little help to very sensitive subjects. Washing after five minutes was useless, merely reducing the rash's severity in five volunteers and making no difference for the other four.

Bonding time depends on several variables, including the potency of the substance, the thickness of the skin, the ambient temperature, and the age of the victim. The attack occurs in the epidermis, just below the cuticle or stratum corneum, in the epithelial cells of the layer that replenishes that cuticle. To reach them, the oil must penetrate the barrier of horny keratin cells that chiefly make up the stratum corneum. Rashes seldom appear on the palms of the hands and soles of the feet where that layer is thickest, but occur readily on thinner skin, like the webs between fingers, the face, eyelids, and the inner arms. The hands may spread the oil to other, more vulnerable parts of the body.

Urushiol dermatitis works faster on warm days because the pores of the skin open and help urushiol to penetrate, because the oils in perspiration may soften or partially dissolve it, and because people usually wear less protective clothing on warm·days or, wearing protective clothing, get the oil under their clothes where perspiration spreads it. Swedish botanist Peter Kalm claimed to be sensitive to poison sumac only during warm weather, when he perspired. Finally, the delay between contact and a rash lengthens as people and their immune systems age. Children under five, who are seldom outside, rarely get it, although between five and 10 they are likely to become sensitized. The rash is nothing if not capricious. Its intensity in the same individual will seem to vary from year to year. The delay in the rash's onset also lengthens as the time between exposures increases.

Removing the oil calls for speed, but anyone with normal reflexes, good sense, and access to suitable cleansers can make a fair job of it. Even proper removal is a matter of controversy, however, and bad advice abounds. What matters is how effective a cleanser will be. Because urushiol is sticky and tenacious, the approved method for many years was to wash it off with a strong yellow laundry soap. Mild soaps with conditioning oils were dismissed as worse than useless, because they merely soften the urushiol and spread it around. Strong soaps saponify it—that is, turn it into more soap—and lift it off the skin. Practice, however, usually falls short of theory. Walter C. Muenscher, professor of botany at Cornell University, outlined the following cleansing method in the 1930s. The best practice then consisted of washing and rinsing the skin very thoroughly several times in hot water with a strong, alkaline kitchen or laundry soap. These were then available under a variety of brand names. They were also known as "yellow laundry soap," of which Fels Naphtha® was the commonest. He stressed lathering heavily and rinsing off repeatedly. Three or four washings were a minimum. He advised against soaps containing moisturizing oils because urushiol is soluble in oil. Dissolved in the soap's oils it will then spread to other parts of the skin.

This old method has several deficiencies, including age and hot water. Yellow laundry soap disappeared from most of America's laundry rooms decades ago, and many stores may no longer carry it. Even if available, one criticism has been that strong soap saponifies the skin's protective oils, too, increasing vulnerability to urushiol spread around from ineffective washing, to later contacts, and to other hazards. It takes three to six hours for the oils to regenerate. Thus, within the last 10 or 12 years this remedy has attracted disfavor, being criticized by more than one dermatologist and a government consumer magazine. Even without abrasives—which should never be used—strong soaps *are* hard on the skin and will irritate it to one degree or another. Other experts argue against strong laundry soap more persuasively because usually it is too little too late, so its harm to the skin may indeed outweigh its potential benefits. Mild soap with conditioning oils, however, is still a bad choice.

Strong laundry soap will at least remove some excess oil and prevent it from spreading around. Any irritation from soap or any cleanser will pale into insignificance beside the rash, and the irritation will vary from skin to skin. A detergent—dish or laundry—works as well (or badly) as soap. Anyone who decides to use laundry soap or detergent should rub not scrub. The soap should do the work, with several latherings and rinsings. Despite Muenscher's advice, wash with cold water. Using warm water for a good lather unfortunately opens the pores and stimulates the circulation, bringing more T lymphocytes to the area. Critics of soap state also that users fail to wash repeatedly with sufficient rinses, and that readily available organic solvents are more effective, despite concerns about skin irritation.

Currently alcohol is favored as an effective and usually handy organic solvent. Alcohol may also pick up and flush out some of the oil that has soaked into the fat chambers of the skin's sebaceous glands where the urushiol migrates after contact. It is even a good follow-up to soap. Maynard M. Metcalf of Johns Hopkins University, writing in 1931, recommended the following method:

Prepare 100 or more pinches of cotton and a shallow bowl of 70% to 95% strength alcohol. That's enough for two patches the size of, say, an oreo cookie. More oil calls for more swabs. Dip a small pinch of the cotton in alcohol, sop up the urushiol, and discard it. Don't let the alcohol dry and don't use the cotton more than a few moments. Throw it away almost at once. Dried alcohol just redeposits the oil on the skin and spreads it. Repeat the process about 50 times for a small patch of urushiol. Don't rub at first, just sop it up. After sopping about 30 times, rub well before throwing away the cotton. Finally, rub vigorously with the alcohol and cotton to get the poison out of the skin's pores. If rubbing breaks small blisters, the urushiol in them will be more readily removed. The alcohol will also sterilize—but irritate—the surface.

Taking time to tear off 100 pinches of cotton may not be the best use of the brief time for getting the oil off quickly, but it won't hurt to count swabs while pinching and daubing.

Briefly, in the early 1950s, technicians at the University of California's Gilman research laboratory used a swab of liquid air to burn off the blistered skin, much as it is used now to lift off suspicious moles. They proposed the process also as a treatment for ringworm. It vaguely recalled tribal treatments of skin defects with poison ivy and oak, bringing matters just short of the full circle. The treatment is no longer used for urushiol dermatitis.

Powerful solvents like gasoline, kerosene, turpentine, and lacquer thinner (which contains acetone), were reviled for years as bad choices, stripping the skin's oils right off and irritating it. Today, however, experts advise their use up to four hours after contact to remove urushiol molecules, especially from the tiny fat chambers of the skin's sebaceous cells. At least one expensive cleanser now on outdoor-store shelves is simply crude gasoline. There are cheaper options.

Prepackaged towelettes, which come soaked in a mild detergent, can remove some oil and are especially useful on trips to clean off pets' fur. They are not very effective for removing it from skin, however, and a later cleansing with alcohol or a similar solvent should follow. The working portion of the towelette should be changed often to keep it from spreading the oil.

Cold running water by the gallon is probably the best and handiest first aid. Urushiol is very slightly soluble in water and forms tiny colloidal globules, which a little water will spread around but a lot will carry off. Medical opinion now deems water as effective—or ineffective—as washing with strong soap. If done within about three minutes, it beats soap. Cold water closes the skin's pores and inactivates urushiol's chemical reaction a little by oxidizing the molecules. Just turn on the water and keep it on as long as local water shortages reasonably permit, or use a pond or running stream. Adding bleach or hydrogen peroxide hastens oxidization.

Doctor Epstein at U.C. San Francisco has recommended cold water followed by alcohol to pick up some of the remaining oil. Merely oxidizing the oil may not completely deactivate it. A few years ago, Julia F. Morton, a botanist at the University of Miami, grubbed out what she later realized were poison ivy roots. When she immersed her hands in a Clorox solution to bleach a garment, black marks appeared instantly on her palms and could not be removed by scrubbing with household cleanser. She next used her hands to lather her neck, which 12 hours later reddened and erupted in a prickly rash and blisters.

Also, Dr. Alan Chovil, Director of Communicable Disease Control for Santa Barbara County, California, confirmed an Associated Press report of January 1995 that runoff from Southern California's deadly winter storms apparently spread the oil into urban areas. Many Santa Barbara residents who waded in to fight the floodwaters got rashes that emergency-shelter physicians could attribute only to urushiol leached from the abundant poison oak above the city. There was no industrial waste or other allergen in or near the city on which to blame the rashes. At least 20 firefighters were afflicted, and a police officer filed a worker's compensation claim. One resident was said to look like he had survived an attack of killer bees, and another's legs broke out after working in knee-deep water to divert it from an art gallery.

Finally, the rash, or any skin liable to get one, should never be tightly covered, as that will hold in the oil and help it to penetrate deeper.

TOO LITTLE, TOO LATE—THE KITCHEN PHARMACY

If it is too late to remove the oil—that's one minute to several hours, depending on the above variables and the solvent—all the soap, water, alcohol, or gasoline in the world won't prevent a rash. Even if some oil was removed, enough may remain to require a counter-irritant, a palliative.

Many victims probably do not notice touching the plant, and a full-blown outbreak—beginning with red streaks where the plant brushed—is the first hint of the encounter. If so, there is a tendency in the teeth of the rash, to grasp at straws or worse for relief, particularly at night when sleep has become a distant hope. Remember that an average case will last 14 to 21 days—and nights—or more. In these circumstances, some people, amazingly, not only admitted to trying the following remedies but even reported that they worked. At least they were not fatal to the reporter. Among the outlandish, foolish, and horrifying "cures" (there are no cures) have been ammonia, banana peel, prepared mustard, chlorine bleach, buttermilk, canned pineapple, lysol, gunpowder, strychnine, clear nail polish, hair spray, meat tenderizer, hardwood ashes, green bean leaves, white shoe polish, marshmallows, toothpaste, bacon grease, kerosene, gasoline, externally applied vitamin E, horse urine—or apparently anything within reach that is more unlikely than the last. The May 1857 *Hutchings' California Magazine*, acknowledging gunpowder as a reasonable specific, recommended a steam bath to sweat out poison oak attacks.

One curious treatment is crab or crayfish meat. There may be no scientific basis for it, but the Chinese discovered by at least the 2nd Century, B.C., that crustacean tissues contained powerful chemicals or enzymes that prevented lacquer from polymerizing. So they threw crabs in the paint pot to keep it from drying out. Cherokees reportedly rubbed crayfish meat on their rash, and the Chinese are said to apply a crab meat broth to lacquer rashes. The author is unaware whether anyone has studied the effect of crustacean tissue on urushiol or on the immune response. The only connection may be the frenzied search for any relief by people in the nettles of the itch.

Many of the lay pharmacopeia's anti-urushiol salves, tinctures, solutions, and poultices are astringents, usually tannic acid or the like. Astringents cause blood vessels to contract, offsetting somewhat the swelling caused by the immune response, stanching the lymphatic ooze, and helping dry up the blisters. Since these potions usually are not sterile, they should be kept away from open blisters. Strong black tea is probably the commonest household source of tannic acid.

Other sources of vegetable astringents are: alum root, amaranth (pigweed), bayberry bark, buckthorn, cinquefoil, ephedra (Mormon tea, ma-huang, squaw tea), gnaphalium purparium, gold thread, golden rod, grindelia (gum plant), Labrador tea (wild rosemary, James tea, marsh tea), madrone, manzanita, mouse ear (hawkweed), myrrh, oak bark, plantain, ragweed, sanicle, septfoil, sumac berries, sweet fern (sweet Cicely, meadow fern, spleen-wort bush), tansey, water-lily root, witch hazel, wild geranium root, wild indigo, and probably most of the other herbal lotions, salves, and tinctures said to resist the assault of the T cells. Sandra J. Baker's *Poison Oak and poison Ivy: Why It Itches and What to Do* provides recipes and directions for over 100 folk medications.

The most praised plant palliatives, claimed truly to neutralize the rash, are jewelweed and plantain. Since many claim extraordinary results for them, they merit a few words. Common plantain (*Plantago major*) and buckhorn plantain (*Plantago lanceolata*) arrived in North America and went west with European settlers. They have evolved into numerous subspecies but generally resemble the illustrations on these pages.

Treatment involves crushing the leaves of either variety to release the pale green sap and daubing it on the rash. The juice dries and the green stain vanishes. Depending on who reports on it, relief lasts for 24 to 48 hours. Some writers recommend keeping the plantain sap moist. One writer, David W. Bradshaw, associate professor of horticulture, Clemson University, Clemson, S.C., claimed in a 1993 issue of *Fine Gardening* that the remedy stopped the

Common or broadleaf plantain

itching and removed his rash within 48 hours. Bradshaw reportedly sets aside a part of his backyard for a medicinal plantain crop. Most people consider them weeds and try to extirpate them from their yards. Often plantain grows near poison oak and ivy, an altogether convenient arrangement. Both plantains are evergreen perennials, potentially available for year-around treatment, climate permitting. If plantain is one weed the garden lacks, The Cook's Garden sells it as a salad green. (Catalog $1.00, P.O. Box 535, Londonderry, VT 05148). In May 1992 T. Paul Misenko, a retired preacher and nursing home administrator in Bristolville, Ohio, received patent No. 5,011,689 for an extract of plantain sap, which he claimed would relieve the itch permanently upon application.

Buckhorn plantain

The juices of crushed jewelweed (*Impatiens pallida* and Impatiens *biflora*), of which *I. biflora* is illustrated here, reputedly equal plantain's remedial power. A common weed in the eastern United States, jewelweed's genus is *Impatiens* and it is called touch-me-not because the seeds explode from the ripe seed pod when touched. Its waxy coating causes water to bead up like gems on the leaves. The juicy stems look almost glassy. *Pallida*, a deep-shade variety common to stream banks and in other damp spots, has single pale lemon-yellow flowers that bloom from July to October. *Biflora*, which blooms from early June through September, takes more sun and its double, mottled butter-yellow and red-brown blossoms appear in shady or sunny moist places.

Jewelweed

Jewelweed's efficacy has its partisans; others back plantain. But jewelweed like plantain has been given no controlled tests. The nearest to a test, reported in the June 1974 issue of *Organic Gardening*, was administered by a registered nurse in Michigan. To one itchy leg of a boy who had strayed into the poison ivy patch at a YMCA summer camp she applied a corticosteroid and to the other jewelweed sap. She claimed that jewelweed relieved the itching and removed the rash in two days. There was no report on the corticosteroid's effect to say nothing of its strength, formulation, time of application, or whether the experiment was repeated.

Accepted practice is to daub crushed jewelweed juice or an extract, on the rash or to add the juice of about a pound of jewelweed to bath water. To make the extract, boil the sap to half its original volume. The strained extract can be applied fresh or frozen in ice trays and kept in plastic bags for later use.

leading to the mining towns, and especially, near the cities of Sacramento, Marysville, and Stockton, where the teamster, the pleasure rider, and the traveler, halts to water his stock, or "take a drink."

THE POISON OAK.

THE POISON OAK.

This subject has elicited more attention, and invited more examination than we supposed it probable, when the first article appeared upon it, in this Magazine. Letters upon letters, of inquiry, and for information have poured in upon us ; some telling us of its inconvenient and painful effects with its accompanying symptoms ; others relating the particular kinds of treatment, which have been successful to them, individually, with a variety of questions as to what it is ? how to avoid it ? what is a certain cure for it ? etc., etc.

To satisfy these inquiries, in some measure, we renew the subject, giving some illustrations of the shrub, and its

effects, in hopes that, although we do not profess to be physician extraordinary, to this class of persons and cases, we may nevertheless diffuse information of value to those affected by it.

For ourselves we may say that we can handle it, and even eat it, with impunity, as it produces no effect whatever upon us ; but we regret to say it is not thus with all.

In the early part of last month, we saw a person almost blind from its effects, and with his entire face, and portions of his body, very much discolored and swollen. In this condition he was recommended the "sweating" process, adopted and practiced by Dr. Bourne, the Water Cure physician of this city. The following statement, from Mr. M. Fisher, will distinctly explain itself.

I was poisoned by contact with Poison Oak, February 22d, 1857, at three o'clock, P. M. At ten o'clock, P. M., 24th, my condition was very distressing as shown by the *first* portrait, then taken, when I was rapidly becoming blind. The *second* portrait shows my improved state *two and a half* to *three hours later*, *after a thorough sweating.* The *third* portrait was taken at forty-eight hours later than the first one, and now I am entirely cured of a very severe affection which was rapidly getting worse, and exhibiting its effects all over my person; *without* medicine or any other than the mode above stated, only three baths. During the year 1853, the Poison Oak caused me partial blindness nearly one month; and total blindness for several days, with much suffering.

Now we give the above, simply to show

EFFECTS OF THE POISON OAK.

The May 1857 issue of Hutchings' California Magazine.

that a good sweating, and the drinking freely of cold water, with the application of cloths, saturated with warm water, to the head and face, can be practiced by any one with the greatest safety and efficiency.

" Any mode (says the *Alta*) of taking a vapor bath will do, either by means of steam admitted to a tight box, or by placing the patient under blankets, and heating the water with hot stones ; or other convenient plan, so that it be effectual, and allow the patient's head to be exposed to the air, avoiding the necessity of breathing the hot and vitiated steam.

" From having witnessed its effects, we recommend the foregoing as a simple and efficient process for overcoming this troublesome disorder, to all such as may unfortunately require its aid.

There are some afflicted so severely, as to induce protracted illness, often blindness, and sometimes even death. We have frequently known it to baffle the treatment of physicians for weeks and months, subjecting the patient meantime, to great inconvenience and suffering. We have, therefore, thought it worth while to give the

AFTER A BATH OF THREE HOURS.

public the benefit of a mode of cure, applied in a case that recently came under our own observation ; and which seems alike simple, speedy and efficacious."

Some have used gunpowder with effect,—others alchohol,—others strong ley—and who have become cured by rubbing the parts affected, although the " sweating " process seems to us, the most natural.

" I suggest a remedy for the pustular eruption," writes a gentleman from Umpqua City, Oregon, " produced by the poison oak :—take sulphate of iron, ten grains ; laudanum, half an ounce ; water, one ounce—mix and apply to the diseased surface, constantly, by means of soft linen, saturated with the solution. If the eruption is persistent, with sympathetic fever, take salts in aperient doses, and one grain of sulphate of iron, internally."

Too much care cannot be used when riding or walking near this poisonous shrub, especially by those persons who are most easily affected. It is also very desirable that a remedy should be applied as speedily as possible after its effects are first felt,—thus saving much annoyance and inconvenience.

CURED.

Steam power presumably overcomes the rash.

Lacking controlled experiments to confirm their effect, we cannot endorse the use of any of these substances. Other than the astringent in their juices or fibers, there is probably nothing magic, mystical, or even efficacious about them. The best medical opinion on urushiol dermatitis is that these folk remedies have a placebo effect. That is not to be discounted for an ailment that for so long yielded so little to efforts at control. Placebos have produced reasonably consistent 30- to 40-percent positive responses in such diverse settings as lowering urushiol sensitivity to certain kinds of cancer therapy. As long as users take precautions against infection, there is no reason not to give them a try. At very worst, they are harmless diversions.

OVER THE COUNTER AND INTO THE FRAY

The problem with an herbal remedy, of course, is to identify it. We who no more recognize the cure than the culprit may prefer to visit the druggist for commercial solace like aluminum acetate, tannic acid, zirconium oxide, iron chloride, and potassium permanganate. If so, take heed, as many of these bear their own venom. Zirconium oxide is perhaps the worst because it can cause an allergic response of its own. Iron chloride is not much better. Potassium permanganate is an antifungal agent that is very strong and toxic, and leaves a durable brown stain. Further, the oxidizing properties of these compounds are not much better than water.

A few decades ago, Albert M. Kligman, M.D., professor of dermatology at the University of Pennsylvania School of Medicine in Philadelphia, studied some three dozen over-the-counter medicines and concluded that none seemed to work better than the old standby, calamine lotion. It provides no real benefit, but evaporates with a cooling sensation, leaving a layer of pink powder to protect the skin, dry up blisters, and relieve the itching. Calamine is 98 percent zinc oxide and 0.5 percent ferrous oxide for color. Suitable for people of all ages in a 25 percent concentration, it has had a long, unblemished clinical career. It lubricates, protects the skin from dryness and the elements, is safe even if swallowed, and causes no complications when externally applied. Concentrations up to 40 percent are available in some ointments. Its absorbency makes it best for bad cases of oozing blisters, but it can irritate rather than soothe when the skin turns dry and peels. Since November 1993, the FDA has classified calamine as safe but not "effective" against urushiol dermatitis, because it merely relieves the symptoms. It cannot be sold as a poison ivy, etc., specific.

Some calamine lotions contain alleged counter-irritants like menthol, phenol, and camphor to cool and anaesthetize. Beware of phenol and camphor. Extracted as a constituent of coal tar in 1834 (thus also called carbolic acid), phenol can be synthesized from benzene and is available from other organic materials. It was the disinfectant that Lister used. It is also extremely toxic. Swallowing half an ounce of concentrated phenol can be fatal, and slightly weaker concentrations can lead to general physical collapse. Applied topically in concentrations above 2.0 percent it may cause skin to peel and die; and—absorbed readily through rashes, injured skin, or membranes—it can cause systemic poisoning. More dilute solutions are safe but useless. Camphor smells good but reportedly has little therapeutic effect. It will irritate skin in concentrations above 2.5 percent. Below that it is safe but little else. Avoid calamine lotions with mixtures of diphenhydramine or promethazine, analgesics and antihistamines, as they can cause their own dermatitis. Benzocaine, dibucaine, tetracaine, and most other topical (externally applied) "caines" can also cause allergic responses. Antihistamines are useless against the rash because too few histamines are released in the response for an antihistamine to make any difference. The drowsiness it induces, however, may be desirable. Aspirin and the like are reportedly useful as placebos.

Among other general compounds to relieve discomfort are cold compresses of boric acid, which while lethal to insects, is mild enough when very dilute for humans to use in eye drops. Another is Domeboro® astringent solution. A one-ounce packet of Burrows Solution® (aluminum sulfate and calcium acetate) dissolved in pint of water can be used in a wet dressing applied often to keep the area moist. Also common is Aveeno®, the principal ingredient of which is oatmeal. Real oats are cheaper. Just tie a cup or two in a cloth and take a bath with them in lukewarm water, or bathe the part, occasionally squeezing the bag or sponging the rash with it. Take care, as the oats will make a bathtub more slippery than usual. A few sources recommend cornmeal, cornstarch, and bran as non-oat stand-ins; and some report relief in vinegar or bicarbonate of soda as bath additives.

The ultimate palliative, almost too farfetched for belief, is to soak the rash for 10 or 20 seconds in very hot water, just short of scalding. People who have tried it report that, once past the intense smarting, relief lasts for up to eight hours. One theory is that the heat exhausts several hours' supply of nerve-irritating enzymes in a few intense seconds. It might even buy a night's sleep. If possible, dip the affected part in the hot water. Otherwise, take a hot bath or shower. Be careful to avoid the obvious risk of scalding, especially when blisters appear.

Physicians have dismissed over-the-counter medications of 0.5% to 1.0% cortisone as too weak to do any good. Prescription varieties of corticosteroids are effective if used early enough, usually within 48 hours, but cortisone's side effects, the foremost of which is a lowered resistance to disease and infection, are disturbing enough to compel a search for a better control. Administered in excess, it may cripple the adrenal gland for up to nine months. Other effects include increased blood pressure, retention of salt, the onset of latent diabetes, impaired wound healing, the disruption of pregnancy, impaired growth in children, swelling of the face and neck, large loss of body protein, masculinization of women's features, and a capacity for intensifying or even reactivating a variety of disorders, including tuberculosis, peptic ulcer, hypertension, some heart conditions, most psychiatric ailments, and nearly all infections. It is truly a remedy that can be worse than the disease and must be used cautiously and under a physician's direction.

In the later stages of the rash, after the skin has peeled and begun to crust over, it is all right to apply a moisturizing cream or lotion to control dryness and residual itching.

Common sense is often missing from bouts of urushiol dermatitis, but this may help summon a little reason during the event. For those only slightly or moderately sensitive the familiar home remedies may control the typical attack. The very sensitive, however, should get medical assistance immediately and follow their physician's directions precisely. So should anyone with a worse than normal attack. One

company library, concluded that the company made a compound superior to any being tested. He submitted spray-on samples. The compound contained a high concentration of the activated organic clay also used in deodorants. Test results showed that it protected just over 95 percent of subjects. The test did not report the wash-off times, so it cannot be compared to those in the 1992 study. After the test, United Catalyst spun off a pharmaceutical division to take the product through FDA testing. The barrier lotion was nearing approval at the time of writing, nearly 10 years after the test, but could not yet be released for sale.

Barrier creams and lotions are not cure-alls. They cannot block out all the urushiol; but they can reduce a rash's severity. The mildly sensitive may get no reaction at all and the moderately sensitive may get a lighter case. Perspiration and friction can reduce their effectiveness. All should be washed off as soon as possible, otherwise the molecules eventually will work through to the skin. Many preparations come with a cleanser to remove the barrier with its embedded urushiol molecules. The cleansers are either based on strong detergents or organic solvents like gasoline, alcohol, acetone, etc., which may be cheaper and more accessible from ordinary sources.

the oats will make a bathtub more slippery than usual. A few sources recommend cornmeal, cornstarch, and bran as non-oat stand-ins; and some report relief in vinegar or bicarbonate of soda as bath additives.

The ultimate palliative, almost too farfetched for belief, is to soak the rash for 10 or 20 seconds in very hot water, just short of scalding. People who have tried it report that, once past the intense smarting, relief lasts for up to eight hours. One theory is that the heat exhausts several hours' supply of nerve-irritating enzymes in a few intense seconds. It might even buy a night's sleep. If possible, dip the affected part in the hot water. Otherwise, take a hot bath or shower. Be careful to avoid the obvious risk of scalding, especially when blisters appear.

Physicians have dismissed over-the-counter medications of 0.5% to 1.0% cortisone as too weak to do any good. Prescription varieties of corticosteroids are effective if used early enough, usually within 48 hours, but cortisone's side effects, the foremost of which is a lowered resistance to disease and infection, are disturbing enough to compel a search for a better control. Administered in excess, it may cripple the adrenal gland for up to nine months. Other effects include increased blood pressure, retention of salt, the onset of latent diabetes, impaired wound healing, the disruption of pregnancy, impaired growth in children, swelling of the face and neck, large loss of body protein, masculinization of women's features, and a capacity for intensifying or even reactivating a variety of disorders, including tuberculosis, peptic ulcer, hypertension, some heart conditions, most psychiatric ailments, and nearly all infections. It is truly a remedy that can be worse than the disease and must be used cautiously and under a physician's direction.

In the later stages of the rash, after the skin has peeled and begun to crust over, it is all right to apply a moisturizing cream or lotion to control dryness and residual itching.

Common sense is often missing from bouts of urushiol dermatitis, but this may help summon a little reason during the event. For those only slightly or moderately sensitive the familiar home remedies may control the typical attack. The very sensitive, however, should get medical assistance immediately and follow their physician's directions precisely. So should anyone with a worse than normal attack. One that causes unusual swelling, dizziness, hard breathing, uneasiness, nausea, or other severe symptoms, requires medical attention, as does one that covers more than 20 percent of the body, causes severe facial swelling, or does not improve over the standard two to three weeks. Urushiol responses have been fatal and are not to be trifled with.

BARRIER CREAMS—BOTTLED COVERAGE

Barrier creams and lotions to keep urushiol from reaching the skin in the first place have been available since the 1940s in bentonite, tyrosinase, kaolin, and organo-clay compounds. Test methods to measure the effectiveness of each have varied so much, however, that one study's results bear little comparison to any other's. One from the early 1980s described a barrier cream that seemed to protect over 90 percent of subjects if washed off within eight to 12 hours of application. A 1992 test found that the same preparation protected just under 60 percent after a four-hour wash-up. On the other hand this product, now called Stokogard Outdoor Cream® (Stockhausen Corp., 2408 Doyle street, Greensboro, NC 27406; 1-800-328-2935), provided the best protection in both tests. Products that did nearly as well were Hydropel® (C & M Pharmacal, Inc., 24047 Dequindre, Hazel Park, MI 48030; 1-800-459-8663) and Hollister Moisture Barrier® (Hollister, Inc., 2000 Hollister Drive, Libertyville, IL 60048; 1-800-323-4060). All seemed to prevent a rash by keeping the urushiol molecules from reaching the skin, rather than by bonding with them chemically. The researchers hypothesized that the urushiol molecules, which ordinarily slip between the keratin cells of the skin's cuticle via intercellular fat globules, were attracted to and slowed by the heavy oils in the barrier creams. Stokogard also contains a linoleic acid dimer used in cutting oils to reduce machinists' contact dermatitis.

Only one company has sought approval of its barrier lotion under the U.S. Food and Drug Administration (FDA) testing procedure. A study in 1986 at U.C., San Francisco, notably of aluminum chlorhydrate, the active chemical in antiperspirants, suggested that it bonded with urushiol molecules and deactivated them. Tony Schulz, a chemist with United Catalyst Corporation in Louisville, Kentucky, learned of the study in its later stages and, checking a reference in the

6

For every evil under the sun,
There is a remedy or there is none.
If there is one, try and find it,
If there is none, never mind it.

—Mother Goose Rhyme

PROSPECTS FOR RELIEF

ONG BEFORE medical science began to seek an anti-urushiol pill or injection, the impulse to build up a resistance was firmly embedded in North American folkways. Its most dubious expression has been in the annual spring snack of poison oak or ivy leaflets to introduce their "weak new juices" into the system. The hope was to induce a tolerance of the plants' oils as they matured and strengthened. Many, including wild-asparagus stalker Euell Gibbons, insisted that eating bits of young poison ivy or oak plants for a few weeks each spring would ensure a leathery resistance to their sap. Gibbons prefaced this by admitting that he had never been troubled much by the plants. Then, chasing a "rumor" from the Pacific Northwest, he told of a family who attributed their lifelong freedom from poison ivy rashes to munching three leaflets a day as soon as the plants began to grow in spring.

Gibbons' assurance, like the others, is an exercise in *post hoc, ergo propter hoc.* For all but those truly insensitive to urushiol leaf-eating is a highly dangerous act. It is, in Berton Roueché's words, "a pernicious and persistent delusion." DO NOT DO IT! The oils—wherever and whenever found in the plant—are the same all year around. They are, in fact, most dangerous in the spring when the tender leaves are easily bruised. The oils in the first leaf ingested may exceed the body's normal level of tolerance and provoke a serious internal attack. Only the stamens and pollen of the flowers are harmless, and they have no preventive properties. A salad of tender new leaflets is as bad as a bale of old branches and can cause very disagreeable, if not fatal, consequences. Medically recorded effects include severe gastroenteritis (inflamed stomach and intestinal linings), respiratory distress, hemorrhoids, and headaches, as well as kidney damage or kidney failure resulting in death. Their least mischief can be a rash at both ends of the digestive tract.

The safest recommended folk preventive was thought to be drinking milk from goats fed on the local poison ivy or oak. Even scientists speculated that it might provide effective protection. Unfortunately, University of California researchers found recently that the milk from goats set to clean out a poison oak patch contained no detectable urushiol. Their hypotheses are that the urushiol molecules either bond to the milk proteins, bond to other tissues on the way to becoming milk, are oxidized in the liver, or pass out in the urine bound to dead body cells. Claims of a milk-induced resistance may come from people who milked their own goats and, like the luckier cashew workers, got it from repeated exposure to the oils on their goats' fur. So, unless there are other factors present in the milk, this folk remedy, while nourishing, may be as worthless as it is harmless.

The folk principle seemed at least to be on the right track. The scientific search for a preventive has involved chiefly introducing urushiol in gradually increasing doses to induce the immune system to tolerate the oil. While this method produced some tolerance almost from the beginning, finding an effective inoculant that was also safe has been an elusive goal.

One obstacle has been that, since urushiol is an allergen, the sought-after drug must work in a way diametrically opposed to how other vaccines work.

A measles vaccine, for instance, introduces a weakened measles antigen into the body, inducing it to make a special *antibody* to protect against measles. The new measles-specific antibody easily subdues the weakened antigen. It becomes a measles-specific immunoglobulin G (IgG). Then, with a few thousand of its kind, it remains for life to multiply quickly for immediate protection if full-strength measles antigens ever appear. The normal, healthy body eventually makes millions of antigen-specific IgG's, with or without the help of vaccines.

By contrast, an anti-urushiol drug must somehow induce the body to block its normal antigen-fighting response—but only for urushiol's neoantigen. "No immune response" means "no rash;" so the drug needs to stop the response or replace it with an effective, but benign, new one. An effective anti-urushiol shot might, for example, cause IgG's to neutralize the allergen before the T cells can begin their destructive campaign. Some ordinary allergics appear to produce enough rash-specific IgG on their own to inhibit urushiol dermatitis. One hypothesis is that somehow the IgG's prevent the T-cell receptors from identifying the urushiol neoantigens.

A common treatment for allergies generally has been to desensitize patients with gradually increasing amounts of the allergen up to a "maintenance dose." For years treatments with shots or capsules of urushiol have induced at least a partial blocking response, although how it did so was never exactly known.

One early attempt seems to have been a one-shot, folk-inspired improvisation. In 1942, during World War II, Colonel Sanford William French ordered Sergeant Seymour Shapiro, a peacetime chemist for a New Jersey flavor extracts firm, to gather branches of poison ivy from the backwoods of Fort McPherson, Georgia, and to extract their oils by crushing the leaves and soaking them in alcohol. When the alcohol turned intense green, the solution was filtered, bottled in 50cc vials, and shipped to camps in the Army's Fourth Service Command in the southeastern United States. One-tenth cc of the extract was diluted with 1.0cc of saline solution for intra-muscular injection into troops who had poison ivy rashes.

Between 15 and 30 percent of the Army's summer and fall basic training casualties were from urushiol dermatitis. Although the French-Shapiro extract had enough active urushiol to cause a rash if applied externally, the Army claimed that when injected it desensitized victims' skin and stopped rashes in progress. Colonel French, who was insensitive to urushiol, invented the extract. Injected in Sergeant Shapiro, it gave him a rash.

Later experience showed that urushiol extracts should not be given during an active attack, as they may worsen existing symptoms and cause a systemic reaction. What saved our troops may have been a fortuitous principle of urushiol's chemistry.

The first effective urushiol-based extracts had begun to appear in the 1930s when a chemist in Texas, Hugh Graham, managed to extract urushiol without deactivating any of it. Until that time, extractive agents, including that in the French-Shapiro tincture, contained water. When water deactivated urushiol by oxidizing it, the concentrations would be erratic if not, perhaps, largely neutralized. Once the urushiol was extracted by the Graham method, the solvent was then evaporated and the allergen mixed in vegetable oil. Graham eventually sold his process to Hollister-Stier Laboratories, which became a principal supplier of high-grade urushiol extracts.

During 1953, Dr. Kligman, himself a victim of severe urushiol dermatitis, could be seen on several mornings each week crawling through the shrubbery of Philadelphia's Pennypack Park to gather bunches of poison ivy. At the time he was testing an experimental product and, by using it, got only a slight rash for his efforts. Doctor Epstein, then newly graduated from the University of California's Medical School in San Francisco, assisted in the research before returning to San Francisco in 1957. The inoculant, made from a synthetic urushiol, was tested by injecting increasing doses seven to 15 times into volunteer convicts. It had been synthesized in 1948 by Professor Charles R. Dawson and Dr. David Wasserman at Columbia University. Their financial support came from a manufacturer of cashew-oil products, the Irvington Varnish and Insulator Company, which wanted to protect employees better from its leading raw material.

Doctor Kligman's test results, while promising, had perplexing side effects: hives-like rashes at the site of the last outbreak, anal rashes, and intestinal disturbances. The side effects continued to accompany the treatments for years despite the increasing refinement of extracts and methods. These problems notwithstanding, the extracts did offer relief to highly sensitive victims. Researchers eventually managed to purify the extracts to control the concentration, and in time the urushiol was administered orally for a more accurate dose.

In an experiment to try building up a pre-exposure tolerance, Dr. Epstein gave weekly injections of urushiol and olive oil to children who had not yet encountered the plants. Three to five years after the treatments stopped, however, half the children became sensitized and got rashes.

A report in 1992 by Drs. Kligman, Jere D. Guin, and Howard I. Maibach conceded that research into preventive pills and inoculations had been "less fruitful than anticipated." With injections of urushiol, some subjects were modestly resistant for a year, but many products seemed too dilute to work. Patients who swallowed urushiol had to consume large amounts to become desensitized, but not completely protected, and it lasted only a few months. Building maximum resistance took three to six months but began to decline when treatment stopped. All subjects experienced the above side effects to one degree or another.

Echoing that glum assessment, the FDA's May 1994 *Medical Bulletin* noted that over the preceding eight years 1.7 percent of Americans over 17 years of age had complained of severe reactions to all allergenic extracts, including those of urushiol. Symptoms included itching all over, troubled breathing, flushing, and hives. Even worse, the FDA received reports that, with some 52.3 million injections for that period, 35 patients had died from them. Most of the victims (83 percent) were asthmatic; another had hay fever, hypertension, and cardiovascular disease, and was taking a beta blocker at the time of the injection. The report also cited errors like administering an incorrect dosage and immunization while a reaction was in progress. The toll was 0.7 deaths per million exposures, which, although low, was not acceptable.

Following an advisory panel's 1985 report that all allergenic extracts were too risky, the FDA eventually set new standards for urushiol products. None of the extract manufacturers received approval by the FDA's August 1993 deadline for meeting the standards, however, and the agency ordered all urushiol extracts, both oral and injected, off the market.

Doctor Epstein objected that while the FDA properly ordered withdrawal of the low-content injected extracts, it also cut off the supply of high quality oral products and left patients on anti-urushiol programs to fend for themselves.

CLOSING IN

From almost the first use of extracts to build a tolerance to urushiol, researchers have pursued the source of that tolerance. One clue seemed to emerge from how extracts got the oil into the body. Picked up naturally, urushiol bonds immediately with the skin and does not circulate internally where other immune components can get at and deal with it. Because an oral or injected dose gets urushiol past the skin, its molecules apparently encounter different immune components which can join the response. The problem has been to discover and isolate the internal component that moderates the natural response, and to inject it into test subjects to see if it would prevent rashes without the usual side effects.

Doctors Mahmoud A. ElSohly, E. Sue Watson, and Coy W. Waller, chemists at the University of Mississippi, began to search for a safe, effective inoculant in the early 1970s. Their work led them to observe that once in the bloodstream, some urushiol molecules formed a *conjugate*, or union, with red blood-cell membranes. When injected in laboratory mice, the conjugate did induce a tolerance. They saw the problem as one of getting the urushiol to form the conjugate, free of side effects, by excluding excess amounts of the allergen.

Their first approach was to create the conjugate outside the body and reinject it. Doctor ElSohly reported that while the procedure induced a trouble-free tolerance, it required an elaborate external preparation of blood-cell membranes for injection into a vein. They tried a simpler, cheaper approach: Slow or disable urushiol's action so that it formed the conjugate before it could attach to the skin or other soft tissue. To do this Dr. Watson created an *ester*—that is, replaced the urushiol catechol's acid hydrogen with an acetyl group—for use in an intramuscular shot. The slower-bonding substance, a strained synthetic material, reportedly induced a rash-free tolerance in lab animals as hypothesized. The drug was designed to require a single 20-milligram injection in humans every year, as compared to a series of doses reaching up to 300 milligrams of urushiol-derived extract. The ElSohly-Watson-Waller drug has been offered for commercial licensing; however, clinical testing may take place under private auspices.

Another clue to controlling the rash came from experience with allergy patients. Allergists have long known that patients with hives and eczema seldom get poison ivy rashes. One hypothesis was that their allergies induced "rash-specific" IgG's that blocked the response.

At U.C. San Francisco, Dr. Vera S. Byers, M.D., an immunobiologist, and Dr. Neal Castagnoli, a chemist, speculated that the internal component that limited the rash in urushiol-extract patients was a specialized antibody—that is, an urushiol-specific IgG. In 1974 they began theoretical research into the existence and nature of the antibodies that internalized urushiol molecules might induce.

The likeliest to block the T-cell response was a subclass known as an *anti-idiotype* antibody. In this context, anti-idiotype means "opposed to its own immune response." Specifically, it acts as a counteragent by stimulating T suppressor cells to stop the reaction.

In 1985, to test their theory that an anti-idiotype component would prevent a rash, Byers and Castagnoli enlisted the support of Dr. Epstein, some of whose patients with extract-reduced sensitivity would volunteer their urushiol-specific IgG. By extracting and fractionalizing the immunoglobulins, they succeeded in isolating that component. As they hypothesized, when injected into mice, it stimulated T suppressors and prevented a rash. Initially, they had expected only the anti-idiotype antibody to trigger suppression of the response. Their later investigations showed that both the antibodies and certain other T cells activated the T suppressors.

The inoculant exhibited no harmful side effects, and in 1990 they founded a small company to test and market it. It is now undergoing clinical trials at this date, and the company hopes to begin marketing it in one or two years. It is to appear first as an injection for extremely sensitive and occupationally at-risk patients, then will be available in an oral form.

While prevention of poison ivy, oak, and sumac rashes seems nearer than ever before, there are no guarantees. If the allergen continues to elude control, all we can do when a rash comes is to wait it out as usual. For, as Captain John Smith observed some 385 years ago, its consequences normally "passe away of themselves without further harme. . . ."

Judging under way at the Columbia, California, Poison Oak Show. The master of ceremonies was breaking out in a rash at the time.

A sampling of entries at the Poison Oak Show.

POISON SUMAC (*Toxicodendron vernix*) in summer; note the red midrib and white axial flowers.

Below: Poison sumac with typical leaf shape.

A small poison sumac plant in fall.

EASTERN POISON OAK (*T. toxicarium, quercifolium,* or *pubescens*).
This is a distant relation of poison ivy. It seeks a completely different
habitat. The two rarely hybridize. Note the asymmetrical lobing of the
side leaflets.

POISON IVY (*T. radicans*). Smooth-margined leaves, typical on the east coast, in summer.

POISON IVY (*T. radicans*). Spring leaves showing reddish tinge and smooth leaf margins.

POISON IVY (*T. radicans*). Leaves in fall. Notched margins are common in many parts of the country.

POISON IVY (*T. radicans*). Winter. Coarse root hairs give old vines a hairy-rope look. Any part of any of these plants will cause a rash despite dormancy.

POISON IVY (*T. radicans*). Clusters of poison ivy berries. They will give as bad a rash as the rest of the plant. Do not eat them.

RYDBERG POISON IVY (*T. rydbergil*). Spring. Note leaflets folded in a "spoon" shape. Leaf margins vary on this variety too.

Rydberg poison ivy in fall.

A nice spread of Rydberg in summer.

WESTERN OR PACIFIC POISON OAK (*T. diversilobum*). Lobed here like a California Valley Oak (*Quercus lobata*) or the like; but lobing and leaf form vary widely.

Spring. Western poison oak. This form has a spring blush.

Western poison oak leaves in fall, happy in partial shade.

WESTERN OR PACIFIC POISON OAK (*T. diversilobum*) in a second-growth redwood grove.

7

Don't let that worry you. Lots of people don't like their relatives.

–Dashiell Hammett, THE THIN MAN

THE CASHEW FAMILY ALBUM

NACARDIACEAE are mostly tropical and subtropical. Like all plants, however, they occasionally emigrate, helped by a human or other agency like birds, winds, or ocean currents. Given half a chance, they will ignore their climatic program and set up in the neighborhood. Because of this limited but observed nomadism and people's cross-sensitization to other Anacardiaceae's oils, we who react to poison ivy, oak, or sumac should have a nodding acquaintance with their relations and try to avoid them.

THE CONTRADICTORY CASHEW

The Cashew Tree (*Anacardium occidentale*), native to Brazil and titular head of the family, can grow 30 feet high, with a spreading crown of dull, blue-green leathery leaves about 6" long. Its virtues may excuse its faults. Although it is strictly a tropical plant, it deserves mention here for its commercial value and the chance that its products may find their way into our lives. Gillis tells of souvenir cocktail stirs from Haiti in the 1950s, shaped like voodoo dolls with heads made from unroasted cashew nuts. They were not only a brief, mysterious source of travelers' dermatitis but had eyes made from rosary-pea (*Abrus precatorius*) seeds, two of which when chewed and swallowed would kill the average adult.

Cashew nut dangling below its apple (the ripened stem).

The cashew fruit, which encases the nut, starts off hard and kidney-bean shaped, hanging below the flower stalk. The stalk swells up to a safe, fleshy and sweet pear-shaped food the size of a fist, which turns white, yellow, or scarlet when ripe. The ripe stalk, is sold commercially as a cashew apple. The "apple" can be made into jam. Its milky juice is also fermented into wine, and the wine distills to a rum-like spirit. The cashew does not grow inside a shell at all, but within the real fruit which hangs below the swollen stalk or "apple." Cracking the fruit releases the nut, which is edible only after roasting to destroy its toxic cardinol, cardol, and anacardic acid. The same oils are extracted from the fruit husk for commercial applications. Its cardol, like that in the mango tree, has a chemical structure like urushiol's and will cause the same rash.

The cashew is economically a very valuable plant. Native Tupís called it the *acaiu* (Aca = nut; iu = producer). The Portuguese modified it to *cajú* (cashew) and spread it throughout their empire, beginning in the early 1500s. The trees soon appeared in Goa, Madagascar, Mozambique and Angola. They thrived in dry, stony soil, and their deep roots controlled soil erosion. Both the apple and nut are staples in native diets.

Its oils and resins resist grease, water, corrosion, fungus, and insects, and protect fine hardwoods. Fishermen smeared their nets with them as a preservative. They were used like oriental lacquer to paint canoes, boats, floors, and wooden roofs. The cashew's anacardic acid kills mosquitos and roundworms, and is used as an insecticide to termite-proof lumber. Since the resins tolerate wide temperature changes, they have been a strategic material for electrical insulation in aircraft since World War II. Despite allergic reactions to their products, there are over 100 industrial patents for them. They are the base for plastics, lubricants, and an indelible marking ink. They are also used in the manufacture of varnishes, paints, typewriter platens, printing ink, automotive and aircraft reinforcements, in heavy-duty brake linings, and to waterproof paper. Currently the market accounts for over 600,000 pounds per year. The oils and resins are a renewable resource and potential cash crop from tropical forests. They do, however, have the family's one little problem.

In 1991, two Japanese chemists testing 16 compounds from the oil discovered that some of the extracts worked well against certain bacteria, in particular those that cause acne and tooth decay. One chemist said that the compounds interfered with the decay bacteria's enamel-eroding acids and had an anti-plaque effect. He predicted that the compounds would prove safe when mixed into toothpaste or mouthwash.

NOT-SO-NICE BRAZILIAN SPICE

One of the more ferocious Anacardiaceae species now in the United States is the Brazilian Pepper Tree (*Schinus terebinthifolius*). Heavily foliaged in coarse, aromatic, evergreen leaves bearing five to nine leaflets up to 3" long, it can form an enormous, dense thicket of tangled, woody stems 40 feet high and wide. When trained to a single trunk, sometimes 20 inches thick, it has a broad umbrella-shaped crown that may grow 26 feet high. Its compact sprays of tiny off-white flowers produce juicy, round berries rich in a resinous and peppery aromatic oil.

The tree spread north via Central America into southern Arizona, southern California, and Florida in the mid-19th Century. Then in 1898, on the first of several occasions, the U.S. Department of Agriculture, for reasons known only to itself, introduced its seeds into Florida. The University of Miami's Dr. Julia F. Morton blames the pepper tree's proliferation, however, on an enthusiast in Punta Gorda who propagated it in the early 1920s and another who promoted it under the misnomer "Florida Holly." Also called the "Christmas Berry," it soon spread widely throughout the state as a source of holiday decorations before being recognized as, not a shrub, but an invasive tree whose formidable tangle of stems and branches defies extermination. Birds have scattered the seeds throughout much of south and central Florida, including the Everglades, and it has displaced native species over thousands of acres disturbed by hurricanes and development.

Unlike poison ivy, oak, or sumac, this one will give a proximity rash. Its highly volatile oil produces dermatitis by vaporizing, especially during bloom. Both the flowers and, in some circumstances, the crushed berries can cause eye inflammation and facial swelling from a distance. Respiratory distress like asthma is common, as is sneezing, severe sinus congestion, and headaches. Highly sensitive people have broken out in head-to-foot dermatitis from attempting to trim pepper tree hedges even when not in bloom. The leaves and berries, when eaten, can cause gastroenteritis and vomiting. A calf that grazed on pepper tree leaves suffered a swollen head and eye hemorrhages. Morton reports a case from 1969 when a 9-year-old boy whiled away his time stripping pepper tree branches of their leaves and fruits while also sticking his fingers in his mouth. He was then seriously ill with vomiting and chills for several hours afterward. Amazingly, some chefs once used the dried berries as seasoning. Morton urges keeping them off the menu.

. . . AND ITS PERUVIAN PAL

The California Pepper Tree (*Schinus molle*), a native of Peru, is an ostensibly benign near-relative of the Brazilian variety. This picturesque, familiar evergreen, susceptible to frost but tolerant of drought, resists fire and adorns many a California mission. Its bright green leaves are fringed with narrow leaflets, and its clusters of creamy summer flowers make pinkish berries. The trunks of old specimens are ornately gnarled with knots and burls, and side branches droop like willows from its heavy main limbs. John D. Mitchell of the New York Botanical Garden, writing in the journal *Advances in Economic Botany*, warns nonetheless that it may cause minor inflammations a little like those of its Brazilian cousin. Mitchell echoes Morton's concern that any species in the family may turn on innocent bystanders. There have been no reported cases of dermatitis, however, from this one.

FLORIDA'S POISONWOOD

The Florida Poisonwood Tree (*Metopium toxiferum*)—native to Central America and the Caribbean—has colonized Florida as far north as Daytona Beach. Linnaeus classified it *Rhus metopium*. Also known as Coral Sumac, Hog Gum, and Doctor Gum, its resinous gum is emetic, purgative, and diuretic. It can grow to 40 high, and has leathery, 6" to 10" long evergreen leaves of three to seven leaflets, and flaky, reddish bark. American Forests' 1994 *National register of big trees* notes a 39-foot-tall poisonwood in Florida's Lignumvitae Key State Botanical Site. Its sap turns black on exposure to air making tarry patches and spots on injured bark and leaves. Its heavy, bright bunches of pumpkin colored fruit develop from greenish yellow flowers. It is among the commonest shrubs of the deep rich lime soil of the pinelands and hammocks of Florida's southern peninsula and Keys. Its seeds were probably blown there by hurricanes from the Caribbean.

Morton reports that specimens growing close to desirable trees often escaped bulldozing, and survived to decorate and bedevil parks and subdivisions. Volunteers from bird droppings can sprout unnoticed in gardens. Shiny young specimens have been innocently transplanted to dooryards and their foliage used in floral decorations. The sap can stain the skin black and produce delayed hypersensitivity reactions, from a mild rash to symptoms requiring hospitalization. The sap has been reported to differ enough from urushiol to cause a special problem. Morton tells of a man insensitive to poison ivy who pulled the vines off an established poisonwood tree and got a rash apparently from the tree. Burning the wood also causes facial and respiratory problems.

Florida poisonwood tree.

THE HEAVENLY MANGO

The Mango Tree (*Mangifera indica*) a native of India, Burma, and Malaysia, is named after the Tamil word *mankai*. Bhuddists and Hindus revere mangos as the Fruit of Heaven. There are hundreds of varieties, a few of which grow in mild regions of California and in southern Florida, where some have gone wild. The tree is a dark, handsome evergreen that sometimes reaches 75 feet in height, although it usually stays stunted and shrubby in California. Its dense and leathery foot-long leaves, usually coppery or purple when immature, have a sweet, often turpentine-like aroma if bruised. Yellow to reddish flowers grow in long clusters at the branch ends. Its oil, cardol, flows everywhere in the tree, including the fruit's rind, but not in the fruit itself. Occasionally cardol drips from bruised leaves onto the rind, making it more reactive.

Morton tells of a young woman who in 1958 put a drop of a seedlng's sap on her arm to verify if it had given her a facial rash. The drop raised a 6" by 4" patch of blisters. The seedling, nearly hidden beneath shrubbery near her back steps, was a young mango tree. Mango trees in Florida, says Morton, are a major cause of respiratory problems during their main blooming season, January through February. The flowers emit a volatile oil that can cause facial burning, a rash, and swollen eyelids. Sensitive people should use care handling and eating mangos. They should, for example, clean the knife used to cut the rind before slicing the fruit.

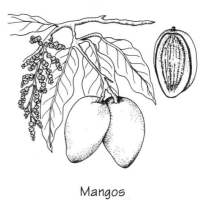

Mangos

GOLDEN RAIN

The Ginkgo Tree (*Ginkgo biloba*), is prized for its autumn foliage, which falls from the tree all at once as a golden carpet around its base. Its leathery, lime green leaves in spring resemble leaflets of maidenhair fern. It can grow to 70 or 80 feet, but most reach only 35 to 50. A probable relic of the Mesozoic era, it was almost extinct but survived because Chinese monks cultivated it. Male trees grow upright, while females are low and spreading. Only males from grafts are available, as the female produces a fleshy, putrid fruit, the nut of which contains the tree's only dangerous part.

HARMLESS SMOKES

The American Smoke Tree or Chittam Wood (*Cotinus obovatum*) is native to the limestone and dolomite bluffs of the southern Appalachians. It extends west into Texas, and is one of three or four species of *Cotinus*. The American variety's wood is light, soft, coarse-grained, and bright orange with a thin, nearly white sapwood. It is very durable in soil and sometimes used for fenceposts. It yields a clear, orange dye, and is hardy as far north as eastern Massachusetts.

Most smoke trees are Eurasian, reaching from southern Europe through the Himalayas into central China. All thrive in poor but well-drained soil and are probably harmless, although there are conflicting opinions and elusive reports of contact dermatitis from the European species, *C. coggygria*.

The American smoke tree

The European Smoke Tree—also called the Venetian Sumac, Velvet Cloak, or Periwig Tree—is grown in North America as an ornamental. It is the hardier variety and produces a much better "smoky" effect. A bushy, urn-shaped shrub about 15 feet tall, spreading nearly as wide, its leaves yield a tannin for high quality leather, and its white sapwood and orange heartwood take a high polish but are suitable only for small objects.

In summer, as *C. coggygria*'s large loose clusters of tiny greenish blossoms fade, their stalks elongate and produce clouds of fuzzy lavender-purple hairs, resembling puffs of smoke. The purpurens variety with purplish leaves makes a darker cloud. The flowers are mostly sterile and their few fruits are tiny, attractive, and poisonous. The foliage colors well in fall but is outshone by the larger American variety, which, while plainer in summer, is the brightest of orange and scarlet fall shrubs.

SHIRT-TAIL RELATIONS

Other economically significant but less familiar species include the Japanese Wax Tree (*Toxicodendron succedaneum*) and the Dhobi, India Ink, or Marking Nut Tree (*Semecarpus anacardium*). The fruit of the Wax Tree is covered with "sumac wax," or Japanese tallow, which substitutes for beeswax and is an ingredient in varnish, ointments and floor wax. Duke and Ayensu report in their *Medicinal plants of China* that this tree's ethanolic leaf extract may have antiviral and anticancer properties. Dhobi is Hindi for laundryman. Dhobis used the nut's dark, insoluble sap to mark garments. Veterans of World War II's China-Burma-India Theater remember those markings from rashes that their dhobi-laundered collars, waistbands, and shirtsleeves gave them.

A NOD TO THE PISTACHIO

The Pistachio tree (*Pistacia vera*) grows to about 30 feet, bearing deciduous leaves with three to five smooth, oblong leaflets. This member of the family is widely cultivated from Afghanistan through Greece, and extensively in California's San Joaquin and Sacramento Valleys. The nuts, about the size of grapes, are salted or roasted for flavor. Lower quality nuts are dyed red to conceal blemishes, but the nuts of every grade are safe for all to enjoy.

The only domestic species, *P. texana*, is native to the limestone cliffs and rocky bottoms of canyons in the Rio Grande Valley that are periodically swept by floods. It is also found in deep narrow ravines along the Pecos River, and around its mouth at Valverde County and northeastern Mexico.

Occasionally it grows as a tree, up to 30 feet high with a short trunk 15 to 18 inches thick. More often it is a large, multi-stemmed shrub. Its leaves usually drop late in fall and may color brilliantly despite mild winters.

The Texas pistachio

With reasonable care the Chinese pistachio (*P. chinensis*) can be trained to grow 60 feet tall and 50 feet wide with beautiful scarlet, crimson, orange, and occasionally yellow fall colors. Its tiny nuts are inedible but crunch cheerfully underfoot in fall when it is planted as a street tree.

8

"Man the mastheads! Call all hands!"
—*Herman Melville,* MOBY DICK

CONTROL OF THE PLANTS

ODERN AMERICANS'
relationship with the *Toxicodendron* genus has been one of skirmish warfare that, especially before the 1940s, occasionally degenerated into a Second Battle of the Marne in miniature. Fairly typical instructions from the 1930s, for example, recommended that

> Poison Ivy may be killed by spraying or otherwise treating the plants as follows: Soak with 3 lbs. of common salt to 1 gal. of water. Or use 2 lbs. of sodium chlorate per gal. of water; of this apply 1 to 1½ gals. per sq. rod. This material can also be dusted on the foliage where it absorbs moisture from the air, goes into solution and is taken up by the plant. Do not let powder or solution touch the

clothing, for when it dries spontaneous combustion may result.

A thorough wetting with kerosene oil is effective but keep the oil off other plants and the surrounding soil if plants are to be grown there.

1 lb. of sodium arsenite to five gals. of water; this is a very poisonous solution and should not be used where cattle might have access to nearby foliage.

Large plants may be killed by cutting the vines at or below ground level and saturating the bases with brine, giving a second application after two weeks. A few drops of crude sulphuric [sic] acid applied to the roots every few days will also destroy the plants within a short time.

Criticism may be unfair at this remove. *Toxicodendron* control through the 1930s was often a desperate matter. The State of Washington appeals court held in 1939 that clearing land of poison oak and ivy was extrahazardous work. During a public works project a hose burst on a flamer used to kill the plants and sprayed a state employee with gasoline, causing his death from burns. It qualified him, the court said, for workers' compensation at the highest rate.

Worse, the plants seemed to respond to eradication efforts with an exponential increase. In 1933 citizens of Brookline, Massachusetts, complained to the Director of Fly and Mosquito Control that there were 58 poison ivy growths in the city, 41 of which property owners had destroyed. In 1934 there were 92 growths, and, in 1935, 230. Through the decade Brookline's health department used every extant method for controlling the plant, including blow torches, table salt solutions, borax powder, fuel oil, sodium arsenite solution, and a highly acid copper sulphate solution. As the 1930s waned, and science developed new controls, people seemed to gain on the plants. In 1942 Brookline turned to ammonium sulfamate, with what it termed gratifying results, and in 1944 began an all-out campaign. The solution, a fireproofing agent, corroded sprayers unless they were thoroughly rinsed with water several times after use and lubricated by running fuel oil through them. In any event, ammonium sulfamate would not poison livestock, and it did not cause spontaneous combustion, sterilize the soil (for long), or envelop civil servants in flame.

On sunny or overcast days, when rain would not wash off the solution, city workers doused the plants once with a coarse spray, which was less likely than a mist to drift onto desirable plants. Then, 36 to 48 hours later, after the leaves turned underside up, they were sprayed again. A final spray 48 hours later killed the surviving leaves. The process destroyed the plants' roots and seeds, as well. After nine years of effort Brookline claimed victory within its borders, even though vigorous specimens still thrived just over the city line.

PREPAREDNESS

There are four ways to deal with the plants. The first three are mechanical, chemical, and biological controls. Poison sumac should not be a backyard problem unless the property in question includes part of a swamp. If it does, the following won't address it specifically, but the rules for controlling poison ivy and oak apply, and they are all qualified by one basic principle: Always be extremely careful.

Uppermost in *Toxicodendron* combatants' minds should be that the targets will fight back. The stems of western poison oak are springy and whip-like. All have wiry, abundant roots that will tangle under foot, around legs, and up sleeves and trousers, all the while seeping urushiol. The author has never had to uproot a large well established poison-ivy or -oak vine or thicket. Confronting either one, however, may warrant calling in professional help or proceeding well armored and warily.

The task calls for serious protection. Suitable dress is long-sleeved shirts, trousers, high-top shoes, eye and face protection, and a hat that covers as much as the season permits. A hard hat with full face shield is a good choice. Otherwise use goggles and wrap the face and neck in bandanas. Tuck in trousers and shirtsleeves. Use heavy washable or disposable gloves, either cotton or leather. Don't remove them until the job is finished. Dressing coolly in a single layer will reduce perspiring. Everything that normally sticks out should be covered. It is no time for concern about what the neighbors may think. The alternative is enduring a rash and its remedies. Further, a deliberate advance into a poison ivy or oak patch is likelier to arouse horror than titillation.

Working on cool, cloudy, or foggy days permits wearing enough to cover up without overheating. Also, chips and sawdust are less likely to fill cool, damp air than when it is hot and dry. William and Helga Olkowski and Sheila Daar—authors of a leading book on pest control and consulting as IPM Practitioners—recommend removing poison ivy and oak during dormancy for these reasons and because the bare plants offer less reactive surface.

Wherever skin is or might get bare it should be smeared with a good urushiol-blocking lotion. Depending on sensitivity, however, even the best barrier cream or lotion may not offer total protection, and an untried product is no guarantee of protection. Take care, too, that the urushiol does not get under clothing and past any barrier cream, where perspiration can spread the oil around. An outdoor advice column from the 1940s once recommended, "Before exposure you may also achieve a measure of protection by applying olive oil to the hands and face. But don't count on it." In fact, don't even contemplate it. Any oil will dissolve the sap and spread it out like a slick.

A later adviser suggested wrapping hands and feet in large plastic bread or newspaper bags held on with rubber bands, then turning them inside out to remove them for disposal. Urushiol is soluble in rubber; it may be in plastic, too, and even thick plastic bags are pretty fragile for heavy-duty yard work. Covering shoes and gloves with plastic could make them easier to clean them afterwards. But it can also promote perspiration. Do it carefully if at all. Consider coating hands and forearms with a barrier cream or lotion before suiting up as a preparation for clean up, but keep in mind that perspiration and friction during the job may reduce the lotion's effectiveness. Whether or not to use heavy cotton gloves during clean up—a final chink in the armor—depends upon individual bravado and how formidable the clump was.

Before touching work clothes again with anything less than, say, a ten-foot pole, launder—or, better, dry clean—whatever is washable. The same promoter of olive oil recommended working in old clothes and burning them afterwards. Assuming local ordinances still allow open burning, consider instead a deep, decent burial, even though the clothing is unlikely to bear enough urushiol to contaminate the smoke. Another possibility is a set of disposable Tyvek® coveralls, which Ben Meadows Company (3589 Broad Street, Atlanta, GA 30341; 1-800-241-6401) sells for around seven dollars. Finally, scrub tools and shoes with hot soapy water and a long-handled brush.

While working, keep an organic solvent, or a bucket of cold water and strong soap or detergent, nearby. If urushiol touches bare skin where no barrier cream or lotion was applied, try to remove it as soon as possible with the soap, detergent, or solvent. After the job, wash off barrier lotions with strong soap or detergent. Good barrier creams and lotions lock up the urushiol molecules but only slow them until a thorough wash-up removes everything.

Once well armored, think before acting. Sheila Daar of IPM Practitioners recommends planning the attack with a simple map of the site to help decide how to deal with each plant and to monitor regrowth once each has been removed.

THE FRONTAL ASSAULT

Mechanical control involves the usual garden tasks of lopping, chopping, hoeing, and digging. Plenty of it. Complete removal means digging out the plant to a depth of 8" to 10" and getting rid of all horizontal runners to a depth of 4" to 6". Otherwise, the plant will spring up again at the same spot or elsewhere along the root system. These roots can spread out for some 20 feet. Using *pi* (about 3.14) times the radius squared (πr^2), that is about 1,200 square feet per mature plant. Grubbing out the plants is practical for only a few plants and only when the soil is moist. In hard, dry soil the roots will break off and send up new shoots. Once the soil is broken, use an ordinary iron rake to grub out the tiny rootstocks, all of which must be disposed of. Removing less than the entire plant is no removal at all, but only a brief setback from which it will return. Even at best, be prepared to follow up, grubbing out shoots for the next few seasons.

If the plants are growing in a hedge or tangled with other foliage, sever them at ground level. Then daub a weed killer on the cut root surfaces with a paintbrush or wick to keep it off the desirable plants. Apply weed killer within an hour of severing, while the plant is still pumping nutrients to the roots. Be careful of dead or dying *Toxicodendron* plants—particularly long, dangling vines and stems. Allow them to wither and return later to remove the less virulent husks; but remember that they stay reactive for years after they are dead.

Mechanical controls

The isolated small plant can be clipped close to ground level then buried or bagged for disposal. Do not compost it, as the urushiol will stay active for a long time. Either grub out its roots, treat them with herbicide, or cover the spot with roofing paper or carpet to prevent regrowth.

Established plants with lots of stems are a special problem. In northern California, Otterstad's Brush Control Service reduces large clumps of western poison oak quickly by "flailing," that is, by chopping the plants into 3- to 8-inch pieces that can be mulched in place. Work crews first use power hedge shears, then a brush cutter with interchangeable saw blades for larger stems. Their hard hats with face shields also provide ear protection against motor noise. Legs are covered in umpires' shin guards, with flaps to their shoes' steel toe caps, and flexible accordion-style PVC pipes strapped on their thighs with Velcro®.

Toxicodendron wood is soft enough to decompose in a few years. A coarse, foot-thick mulch on top of the debris will keep it from people and pets. Regrowth is removed every year after that until the roots die. It can be eaten by goats or spot treated with an herbicide. Herbicidal control is commonest. Small areas can be tarped. Because new shoots present less leaf area, eradicating the plant this way takes longer than treating mature growth with herbicide first and then reducing it mechanically. The above method does offer quick reduction of large plants, however, with complete eradication in a few years.

If grubbing the roots of even a few plants seems arduous and herbicides unsuitable, fight the plants above ground on their own terms, with a war of attrition. When the plant persists, be just as persistent. Chop it down to ground level. Wait a week, 10 days, two weeks. When it sprouts back, chop it down again. Keep repeating the process until the roots exhaust all their stored food, and the plant starves to death. Killing it this way takes patience and perseverance, but it works. The advantage is that the roots need not be grubbed out but only left to shrivel in the ground. Don't relent just because the tide of battle turns against the plant and it appears to be gone. It can appear lifeless for months and spring back to life. Keep watching for it to pop up when and where least expected. Exploring the underbrush for renewed activity calls for caution; the smallest sprout may cause as acute a rash as a sprawling vine.

Daar recommends mulching or planting replacement vegetation as soon as possible, since the poison ivy or oak probably exploited a vacant site in the first place. Eight to 10 inches of mulch may be necessary to keep the plants under control. In some settings, grass can crowd out the new sprouts, and mowing will keep the shoots from leafing out.

Less familiar mechanical controls include covering the poison ivy or oak with roofing paper or a black plastic like Visqueen® to deny the plants needed sunlight. Plastic sheeting is fragile, however, and roofing paper, even old carpet, covered with a mulch is better. Leave the coverings on for the entire growing season. If the poison ivy or oak sprouts the next year, cover it again. Removing these covers once they have done their job requires care, as their working surfaces may pick up some oil. Boiling water poured on the plants, although effective, is practical for only the smallest specimens.

THE CHEMICAL BARRAGE

Chemical controls involve less work, if no less caution, and are not absolutely risk free. In the 1950s 2,4-D and 2,4,5-T, broadleaf plant killers, gained favor because they would eliminate the plants permanently if treatments continued over two years. These compounds have attracted recent government scrutiny, however, as possible carcinogens. Currently, glyphosates and triclorpyls, which affect a gene in plants but do not appear to harm the soil or animals, have become popular as apparently safe controls. Safe is relative. Trusty old ammonium sulfamate, usually one pound to a gallon of water, broke down into nitrogen and sulfur. One of glyphosate's breakdown products is formaldehyde, a known carcinogen and neurotoxin. Glyphosate washed by runoff into streams and lakes travels far and is very toxic to aquatic species. Keep pesticide use to a minimum. For a good discussion of proper spraying practices read *Common sense pest control*, by Olkowski, Daar, and Olkowski.

Chemical control

Glyphosates are sold under names like Roundup®, Kleen-up®, and Knockout®. They come in different concentrations, and it is worth consulting a good nursery or garden center about how to apply them. Glyphosates work very well in summer and fall. Triclorpyls, like Ortho's Poison Ivy & Poison Oak Killer (Formula II)® are best suited for early spring application.

The time to spray is during the active growing season, from April through June or July, with flower and fruiting the optimum stages. Leaves are then at their full extension and pumping hard to the roots. Spray at least before the beginning of dormancy, when the leaves start to turn yellow or red. Some writers advise mixing a surfactant into the spray to improve spreading and adhesion. Take care, as some surfactants are more toxic than a spray's active ingredients. Sprayed plants should be watered normally to help them take up the chemical. The chemicals usually kill the plants in a week to 10 days but may require a repeat application. Be careful to keep the spray off desirable plants. Use a coarse spray on a windless, cool day when there is no chance of rain for 24 hours. Eventually, the leaves will yellow and die, and so will the plant.

Many who distrust chemicals have turned to propane-fired flamers. While flame-throwing may avoid potential chemical hazards, it has not been entirely trouble-free, as the Washington court noted in 1939.

GRAVES AND RUMINATION

Once the plant is reduced to cuttings and shreds . . .

DO NOT BURN IT!

Remember the smoke is very dangerous. Stack, dry, then bag or double bag it in something biodegradable, and bury it deep. Or take it to a landfill and have it interred. Not all landfills will accept poison oak or ivy. If there is too much to bag and bury, compact the pieces onto the ground to decompose and cover them with a 6" to 10" coarse mulch.

One sure and easy way to remove poison ivy and oak plants—and dispose of their remains—is to feed them to goats. The University of California's Agricultural Experiment Station evaluated Pacific poison oak, among other range shrubs, and found it to be good browse for horses, mules, and sheep, as well as goats. Their studies showed poison oak to be nutritious fare. Its crude protein content in new-growth foliage is about 35 per-cent. It declines to 19 percent in late bloom, then falls to 8 per cent when the leaves develop fully and change color. That exceeds the protein in grasses over the same period.

Because goats have been used to open up grazing land, researchers at the University of California's Davis campus investigated using milk goats to clear up poison oak in ranges and recreational areas, as the basis for a commercial dairy industry. With a stall-fed diet of 100% poison oak, goats' milk production declined some, but probably because they ate less in the stalls. Best of all (or worst, for those who anticipated a tolerance-building factor), there was no urushiol in the goats' milk.

The researchers felt that properly managed, that is, staked or fenced to a given area, the goats would not excessively damage non-target vegetation. Ultimately the project ran out of funding, as the purse strings for plant control studies seem to loosen more readily for invertebrate animals (insects and microbes) than for vertebrates. Two of the scientists since have moved to Cornell University, where their studies presumably will continue with poison ivy.

Biological control

For his site management service, Dick Otterstad of Otterstad's Brush Control experimented with Spanish and Angora goats to remove poison oak from suburban lots in the San Francisco East Bay's high brush-fire environment. These breeds were more inclined than milk goats to consume woody shrubs like Scotch broom, bamboo, blackberry, and poison oak and ivy. The U.S. Forest Service has used them since the 1930s to clear fire breaks, and the California Park Service uses them to keep park land open. Despite goats' advantages—complete compliance with brush-fire laws and reducing hazards to work crews from power tools and falling limbs—they were impractical in small applications. Setting up temporary fencing was time consuming, desirable plants had to be screened with additional fencing, and the goats did not completely clear the site.

Otterstad said that some customers specified them as an alternative to herbicides for controlling regrowth of plants that were mechanically reduced. He also used them on large, established sites to

defoliate and debark plants before work crews went in to clear out
the remainder.

CALLING A TRUCE

The fourth way to deal with the plants is more an attitude than a
method. It is to let them be and live with them—what one writer
called a peaceful coexistence. Integrated Pest Management practitioners call it a "tolerance level." If the plant is not in the way or near
a path, a metal barrier sunk in the ground or a trench of ashes will
contain it. As domestic plants, poison ivy and oak are easy to maintain. Recognizing and avoiding the plants is still the best way to
prevent a rash, and keeping samples of the peril in view may make
better sense than attempting their complete removal. An enlightened
tolerance also means less work, with less risk of exposure, too. Like
them or not, poison ivy, oak, and sumac belong to the grand scheme
of things. Besides providing beautiful fall color, they nourish and
shelter a diverse range of creatures. They may have other virtues
worth considering.

9

*. . . lacking both time and inclination, I did not
wait to hear about the afflicted cow, but took
my leave.*

—*Mark Twain, "The Notorious Jumping Frog of
Calaveras County"*

PARTING WORDS

 APANESE POISON IVY
is almost identical to but much less abundant than its American near
relations. William T. Gillis, who noted the disparity, ascribes it to the
preference of all poison ivies for disturbed habitats. It is no accident
that western poison oak, which shares their preference, is the most
widespread and proliferating wild shrub in California. In Japan most
open land has been farmed for centuries or left alone. By contrast,
when gold-mining companies worked California's Sierra Nevadas they
scoured down through hundreds of feet of mountainside—some 50
million years of geologic accretion—to the gold-bearing gravels of
broad Eocene riverbeds. For 30 years, beginning in the middle 1850s,
mining companies used water cannon, some with 9- to 12-inch bores
and 120-mile-an-hour muzzle velocities, to extract over 160 million
ounces of gold from over 1.5 *billion* cubic yards of native soil. The

effluent buried farmland in the Central Valley; the ocean ran brown at the Golden Gate; what remained has been called in modern terms a moonscape. It was site disturbance on the grandest scale, and if nothing else it produced a lot to commemorate at Columbia's annual Poison Oak Show. Poison oak had been similarly absent from California's virgin redwood forests, of which only about five percent remain. The plant now thrives in the range of the other 95 percent, where dense forest no longer excludes it. Far from a purely California phenomenon, the same pattern advanced with us right across the continent from the nation's beginnings. Two of its results were our rising standard of living and an abundance of poison ivy and oak.

This is not to condemn the natural cost of extracting wealth; the greater the wealth, the higher its cost. It seems to be an inviolable economic law, and few of us would abandon civilization because of the expense. Also, far from being a result of the country's development, it seems more reasonable to consider poison ivy and oak natural by-products.

Like all weeds, poison ivy and oak fit into the scheme of our endeavors by setting up in the scars we leave and beginning the slow process of rebuilding the landscape. For this they are admirably suited. They require very little nourishment or moisture (about 10 inches yearly). They are pest-free. They attract and sustain wildlife. Fully one quarter of the diet of red shafted flickers and wren tits is poison ivy and oak fruit during the season; bees make safe honey from their flowers; and they shelter quail and small rodents. Their extensive roots provide superb erosion control—essential in earth building. The Dutch of Friesland province in the northern Netherlands have used poison ivy since the early 20th Century to stabilize dikes. At least one farmer, employing its most notorious property, has sown poison ivy as a hedge to keep pilferers out of his orchard.

As colonizers of raw land, poison ivy and oak are the only ones we can't ignore. They issue what one writer called a "don't touch" message. It gets more insistent the more we dig up the terrain. The real message may be to consider the consequences of our acts—that is, to think perhaps in terms of producing wealth without running up the natural bill.

A small hydraulic mining concern

DEFENDERS OF THE POISON IVY, OAK, AND SUMAC

Not everyone despises the plants, anyway. The English imported poison ivy and oak for their fall color, and introduced them to Australia and New Zealand where they also afford brilliant garden backdrops. For many years the plants were thought to have medicinal qualities. Early settlers, like their native predecessors, used it for eczema, erysipelas, shingles, and warts. Malcolm Stuart states in his *Encyclopedia of herbs and herbalism* that the plants' perceived virtues kept them in some pharmacopeias until 1941. Another source reports that in England poison ivy was used medicinally from 1778 after brushing against it seemed to cure a herpes infection. It was also recommended for paralysis, palsy, acute rheumatism, articular stiffness, incontinence, and skin diseases. The Chinese reportedly used the pulverized dried sap as a tonic and stimulant, and as a specific against coughs and intestinal worms. The seeds were used for dysentery, the leaves for "wasting diseases" and intestinal parasites, and the flowers for the "swelled bellies of children." It also found a place in homeopathic medicine for chicken pox, sprained ankles or wrists, runner's knee and Achilles tendinitis.

Unlikely as the above may appear, urushiol could possess analogs of cashew oil's anti-bacterial properties and the reported anti-viral and anti-cancer principles of the wax tree's ethanolic leaf extract—if those justifications are necessary. Plants with an 80-million year past are probably not an evolutionary mistake. They may outlive us, as they did the dinosaurs.

Perhaps for that reason, as well as for having spent so much time with them, it is only fair to close with a respectful if not good word. The last word, however, can be someone else's. About half a century before Lieber and Stoller set words about poison ivy to music, calling for their ocean of calamine lotion, Jack Killam, self-proclaimed bard of the poison oak, found a metaphor for hard times and survival in its dogged persistence. And his own—

AUTOBIOGRAPHY OF THE BARD OF
THE POISON OAK

'Tis an old joke that Poison Oak
  Is fairest of all flowers.
That orchids rare and lilies fair
  Are good for leisure hours;
But for the dub who'll dig and grub
  Where winter showers soak
There's naught so rare it can compare
  With wreaths of Poison Oak.

. . . .

Without a home, I used to roam
  From Dallas to Medicine Hat—
With saddle and rope, I used to lope
  'Long by the River Platte.
In desert sand, I've help to brand
  For remnant Turkey Track—
O'er mountains high, I helped to pry
  A burro and his pack.
With shovel and pick, I've hit my lick
  For good old Treasure Trove.
With apron and cap, I've had my nap
  By many a kitchen stove.
With a ten-day stake, I've made a
break
  And traveled to Butte and back—
I liked 'em rough—I liked 'em tough
  And drank my coffee black

. . . .

In that bleak land of shifting sand,
  I made more than a ten-day stake,

And put it away for a rainy day
  In a bank and the bank did break.
No crazy bronc', no crafty donk'
  Had played me for a fool,
But with no mount, I took the count
  From the kick of the white mule.
They hauled me far in a baggage car
  To where the doctors live—
And they all said "He'll soon be dead
  "For his stomach is a sieve.
"We think his heart is falling apart,
  "His spleen is hard as a ball—
"As sure as sin, if we start in,
  "We'll have to take his gall."
They took me down in that little
town—
  I watched the snowbirds pant—
They took my parts in little carts
  To their assembling plant,
And made a stall at an overhaul
  And said as a merry joke
"He'll do no harm on a little farm,
  "Way back in the Poison Oak."
For ten long years I've shed no tears
  And I swing a wicked hoe.
I swear I'll grub each deadly shrub
  Wherever the damned things grow.
How could I joke of the Poison Oak,
  Without a bit of gall?

Jack Killam, BALLADS OF THE POISON OAK.

BIBLIOGRAPHY

CHAPTER ONE: First Things

The first chapter is anecdotal and introductory. Most print sources for it are those used for later chapters. Books cited for every chapter invariably provided grist for the others. Although many sources for this chapter were oral, several articles and reports supplemented conversations with people eager to share their poison ivy and oak experiences. Foremost of the print sources are:

Castleman, Michael, "The Itch That Wouldn't Quit," *Parenting* Jun./Jul. 1994, pp. 183-184.

Devich, K.B., J.C. Lee, W.L. Epstein, L.E. Spitler, and J. Hopper, Jr., "Renal Lesions Accompanying Poison Oak Dermatitis," *Clinical Nephrology*, 1975, Vol. 3, No. 3, pp. 106-113.

Ricciuti, Edward R., "Let it Be," *Audubon*, May 1986, pp. 18, 20-21.

Roueché, Berton, "Let it Be," *The New Yorker*, Jul. 2, 1953, p. 16.

Science Newsletter,"Poison Ivy Self-Treatment Nearly Fatal to Boy, Oct. 4, 1947, Vol. 52, p. 217.

CHAPTER TWO: A Social History

The two valuable sources for this chapter were Adolph Rostenberg and Berton Roueché. Roueché writing in the *New Yorker*, and Rostenberg in the *A.M.A. Archives of Dermatology*, set out the broad currents of American and foreign relations with the *Toxicodendron* genus. Following their leads revealed overwhelmingly consistent responses to the plants. Inconsistencies between reports alleging native dietary uses of the plants and most tribes' linguistic and medicinal responses underlie the author's opinion that no one ate the plants except, perhaps, on a dare or possibly a self-immolating kind of put-down. Local tribal sources tell us that stories of weaving baskets with western poison oak were "rumors" and that old-timers often told anthropological field workers what they seemed to want to hear. Texts consulted were:

Bean, W.J., *Trees & Shrubs Hardy in the British Isles* (London, John Murray, [8th rev. ed.] 1976).

Balls, Edward K., *Early Uses of California Plants* (Berkeley, CA, 1965, University of California Press).

Chestnut, V.K., *Plants Used by the Indians of Mendocino County* (Ukiah, California, Mendocino County Historical Society, 1974).

Dickinson, Alice, *Carl Linnaeus, Pioneer of Modern Botany* (New York, Franklin Watts, Inc., 1967).

Douglas, David, *Journal Kept by David Douglas During His Travels in North America, 1823-1827, Together with Appendixes Containing a List of the Plants Introduced by Douglas and an Account of his Death in 1834* (London, William Wesley & Son, 1914; Reprint in facsimile: New York: Antiquarian Press, 1959).

Eifert, Virginia S., *Tall Trees and Far Horizons: Adventures and Discoveries of Early Botanists in America* (New York, Dodd, Mead & Co., 1965).

Frick, George Frederick, and Raymond Phineas Stearns, *Mark Catesby, the Colonial Audubon* (Urbana, IL, University of Illinois Press, 1961).

Hutchens, Alma R., **Indian Herbalogy of North America** (Boston, MA, Shambala, 1991).

Kalm, Peter, *Travels in America*; the English version of 1770, translated by Adolph B. Benson (New York, Dover Publications, 1957).

Leith-Ross, Prudence, *The John Tradescants* (London, Peter Owen, Publishers, 1984).

Merrill, Ruth Earl, *Plants Used in Basketry by California Indians* (Ramona, CA, 1970 [Reprint of University of California Publications in American Archaeology and Ethnology, Vol. 20]).

Morwood, William, *Traveler in a Vanished Landscape: The Life and Times of David Douglas* (New York, Clarkson N. Potter, Inc., 1973).

Reed, Howard S., *A Short History of the Plant Sciences*. (New York, Ronald Press, 1942).

Reveal, James L., *Gentle Conquest: The Botanical Discovery of North America* (Washington, D.C., Starwood Publishing, 1992).

Rostenberg, Adolph, Jr., M.D., "An Anecdotal Biographical History of Poison Ivy," Vol. 72 *A.M.A. Archives of Dermatology*, 1955, pp. 438-445.

Roueché, Berton, "Leaflets three," in *A Man Named Hoffman and Other Narratives of Medical Detection* (Boston, Little, Brown & Co., 1965).

Smith, John, *The General Historie of Virginia, New-England, and the Summer Isles . . . 1584 to . . . 1624* (London, 1624; reprint by Readex Microprint Corp., 1966).

Thalman, Sylvia Barker, *The Coast Miwok Indians of the Point Reyes Area* (Point Reyes, CA, Point Reyes National Seashore Association, 1993).

Whittle, Tyler, *The Plant Hunters* (New York, Chilton Book Co., 1970).

CHAPTER THREE: Toxicodendron Pie

The fun begins. The contributions by William T. Gillis in *Arnoldia* and Kingsbury's book were superb resources. Others occasionally voiced divergent views, but none was wide of Gillis's canon. Mitchell, cited in a later chapter, was particularly valuable for recounting the range and variety of Anacardiaceae worldwide. The titles by Crooks, Frankel, and Leite are good standard works about the North American species.

Crooks, Donald M., and Dayton L. Klingman (USDA Science and Education Administration) *Poison Ivy, Poison Oak, and Poison Sumac* (Washington, DC, U.S. Government Printing Office, rev. ed., 1978).

Frankel, Edward, *Poison Ivy, Poison Oak, Poison Sumac, and Their Relatives* (Pacific Grove, Calif., Boxwood Press, 1991).

Fuller, Thomas C., and Elizabeth McClintock, *Poisonous Plants of California* (Berkeley, University of California Press, 1986).

Kingsbury, John M., *Poisonous Plants of the United States and Canada* (Englewood Cliffs, N.J., Prentice-Hall, 1964). Anacardiaceae contributed by William Gillis.

Leite, Daliel, *Don't Scratch: The Book about Poison-Oak* (P.O. Box 2157, Walnut Creek, CA 94595, Weathervane Books, 1980).

National Register of Big Trees, 1994 Edition (Washington, DC, American Forests, 1994).

Sampson, Arthur W., and Beryl S. Jespersen, *California Range Brushlands and Browse Plants* (Berkeley, CA, University of California, Div. of Agricultural Sciences, Agricultural Experiment Station Extension Service [undated]).

Sargent, Charles Sprague, *Manual of the Trees of North America (Exclusive of Mexico)* (Boston, MA, Houghton-Mifflin, 1905).

Temple, Robert, *The Genius of China, 3,000 Years of Science, Discovery, and Invention.* (New York, Simon & Schuster, 1986).

Periodicals

Bogue, E.E., "The Durability of the Poisonous Property of Poison Ivy, *Rhus Radicans L. (R. Toxicodendron.)*" (Excerpted from *Science*, vol.23, p. 163, 23 Mar. 1894).

Gillis, William T., "Poison-Ivy and Its Kin," *Arnoldia* (1975), Vol. 35, No. 2, pp. 93-123.

CHAPTER FOUR: Urushiol Dermatitis

The sources for much of this chapter were oral interviews with physicians whose practice concentrated on poison ivy and oak rashes. They were kind enough to tolerate my ignorance so that eventually I could relate a very simplified description of how a rash works. At that, this chapter will not make anyone an expert. It may suggest, however, how remedies must work to improve matters. I relied heavily on Drs. Joneja's and Bielory's excellent book on allergy and immunity. Knowledge advances so swiftly in this specialty, however, that such a book must necessarily be out of date as soon as it leaves the printer. I look forward to their new edition. The other sources cited are valuable in their own right and will provide the answers their titles suggest they will.

Edelson, Edward, *Allergies* (New York, Chelsea House, 1989).

Giannini, Allan V., M.D., Nathan D. Schultz, M.D., Terrance T. Chang, M.D., and Diane C. Wong, *The Best Guide to Allergy* (New York, Appleton-Century-Crofts, 1981).

Joneja, Janice M. Vickerstaff, and Leonard Bielory, M.D., *Understanding Allergy, Sensitivity, and Immunity: A Comprehensive Guide* (New Brunswick, NJ, Rutgers University Press, 1990).

MacKie, Rona M., M.D., *Clinical Dermatology: An Illustrated Textbook* (New York, Oxford University Press, 2d ed., 1986).

Mizel, Steven B., and Peter Jaret *In Self-Defense* (San Diego, CA, Harcourt, Brace, Jovanovich, 1985).

Thomas, Lewis, *The Lives of a Cell* (New York, Bantam, 1975).

Periodicals

Crowle, Alfred J., "Delayed Hypersensitivity," *Scientific American* Apr. 1960, pp 129-137.

CHAPTER FIVE: Palliatives & Preventives

The good times roll on as we begin to fight the affliction. Traditional remedies seem to be old wives' and hubbies' tales. Most will do no harm, but some are weird. Even medical prescriptions over the years have wavered back and forth between one and another sound treatment. There really is not much to do, when all is said, except to soothe the troubled part as best one can and wait it out. A bad case really does call for a visit to a physician. Otherwise, calamine lotion and its kind will help keep the hands and mind occupied.

Baker, Sandra J., *Poison Oak and Poison Ivy: Why It Itches and What to Do* (Self, 1979).

California, State of, Department of Industrial Relations, Division of Labor Statistics and Research, *California Work Injuries and Illnesses, 1991* (San Francisco, CA, 1992).

Epstein, William L., M.D., and Vera S. Byers, M.D., *Poison Oak and Poison Ivy Dermatitis: Prevention and Treatment in Forest Service Work* (Missoula, MT, U.S. Department of Agriculture, Forest Service, 1981).

Gibbons, Euell, *Stalking the Wild Asparagus* (New York, David McKay, 1962).

Goodman, Thomas, M.D., *The Skin Doctor's Skin Doctoring Book* (New York, Sterling Pub. Co., 1983).

Muenscher, Walter Conrad, *Poisonous Plants of the United States* (New York, Macmillan, 1939).

Olmstead, R.R., ed., *Scenes of Wonder & Curiosity from Hutchings' California Magazine, 1856-1861* (Berkeley, CA, Howell-North Books, 1962).

Zimmerman, David R., *Zimmerman's Complete Guide to Nonprescription Drugs* (Detroit, MI, Visible Ink [Gale Research], 2d ed., 1993).

Periodicals

Beatty, William H., "A Jewel of a Weed," *Mother Earth News*, Mar./Apr. 1981, p. 8.

Epstein, William L., M.D., "Poison Oak," *Healthline*, Sept. 1994, pp. 10-11.

Grevelink, S.A., "Effectiveness of Various Barrier Preparations in Preventing and/or Ameliorating Experimentally Produced *Toxicodendron* Dermatitis," *Journal of American Academy of Dermatology* (Aug. 1992), Vol. 27, No. 2-Pt. 1, pp. 182-188.

Guin, Jere D., M.D., Albert M. Kligman, M.D., Howard I. Maibach, M.D.,"Managing the Poison-Plant Rashes," *Patient Care*, Apr. 30, 1992, pp. 63-72.

Hecht, Annabel, "The Itch of the Great Outdoors," *FDA Consumer*, Jun. 1986, pp. 22-24.

Kouakou, Brou, David Rampersad, Eloy Rodriquez, & Dan L. Brown, "Dairy Goats Used to Clear Poison Oak Do Not Transfer Toxicant to Milk," *California Agriculture*, Vol 46, No. 3, May/Jun. 1992, pp. 4-6.

Krautwurst, Terry, "The Itch and You," *Mother Earth News*, Issue No. 117, May/Jun. 1989, pp. 118-125.

Mermon, Dick, "Life's an Itch," *Outdoor Life*, Oct. 1987.

Orchard, S., J.N. Fellman, and S.S. Storrs, "Poison Ivy/Oak Dermatitis: Use of Polymeric Salts and Linoleic Dimers for Topical Prophylaxis," *A.M.A. Archives of Dermatology*, Vol. 122, No. 7, pp. 783-786.

Smith, Linda Wasmer, "Rash Actions: New Ways to Protect Yourself from Plants that Make Life an Itch." *Backpacker*, Vol. 22, No. 132, May 1994, pp. 20-22.

Vietmeyer, Noel, "Science has Got Its Hands on Poison Ivy, Oak and Sumac," *Smithsonian*, Aug. 1985, pp. 88-95.

Zamula, Evelyn, "Contact Dermatitis: Solutions to Rash Mysteries," *FDA Consumer*, May 1990, p. 28-31.

Fine Gardening, "Plant Allergies: A Weedy Cure (Plantain) for a Weedy Rash," Sept./Oct. 1993, No. 33, p. 68.

Science Newsletter "Poison Ivy Chemical Now Imitated Synthetically," Mar. 27, 1948, Vol. 53, p. 201.

U.S. News & World Report, "Allergy Warfare," sidebars: "The Complete Guide to Allergy Relief" and "Poison-Ivy Allergies..." Vol. 106, No. 7, Feb. 20, 1989, pp. 69-79.

CHAPTER SIX: Prospects for Relief

Even poison ivy, oak, and sumac may yield to biogenetics. A portion of the material for this chapter came from discussions with researchers working on that esoteric level. The history of creating a preventive shot has had more than its share of blind leads and false alarms; so no one is popping champagne corks yet.

Fine Gardening, "Poison Ivy/Oak Shot," Mar./Apr. 1993, pp. 28, 30.

FDA Medical Bulletin, "Deaths Associated with Allergenic Extracts," May 1994.

The Federal Register, "Biological Products; Allergenic Extracts . . . Revocation of Licenses, " Nov. 16, 1995,Vol. 59, No. 220, pp. 59228-59237.

Time, "Poison ivy cure," Oct. 19, 1942, p. 56.

CHAPTER SEVEN: The Family Album

The author has not encountered any of the rogue flora portrayed in this chapter. He relied entirely on printed reports about their habits and effects. He intends to keep it that way. Different popular authorities vary widely on how virulent one or another Anacardiaceae species is. Some have even recommended them as ornamentals. With Florida the Anacardiaceaes' most favored port of entry, Dr. Morton was a gold mine of acute descriptions of the fiercest of them. Just so they don't sully the entire family, we included a few benign individuals. The sources most relied on here were:

Duke, J.A., & E.S. Ayensu, *Medicinal Plants of China,* Vol. I (Algonac, MI, Reference Publications, Inc., 1985).

Hardin, James Walker, and Jay M. Arena, *Human Poisoning by Native and Cultivated Plants* (Durham, NC, Duke University Press, 2d ed., 1974).

Morton, Julia F., *Plants Poisonous to People in Florida and Other Warm Areas* (Miami, FL, 20534 SW 92 Ct.; Pub. by author; 2d ed., 1982).

Perkins, Kent D., and Willard W. Payne, *Guide to Poisonous and Irritant Plants of Florida* (Gainesville, FL, University of Florida, Institute of Food and Agricultural Sciences, Florida Cooperative Extension Service Circular No. 441, 1978).

Simon and Schuster's Guide to Trees (New York, Simon & Schuster, 1977).

The Wise Encyclopedia of Cooking (New York, William H. Wise & Co., 1948).

Periodicals

Mitchell, John D., "The Poisonous Anacardiaceae Genera of the World," *Advances in Economic Botany*, Vol. 8, 1990, pp. 103-129.

Olaya, Clara Ines, "Caju/Marañon/Merey/Acaiu/Cashew Nut," *Américas* 42:3, 1990, p. 52.

CHAPTER EIGHT: Control of the Plants

Weeding a garden is hard enough work without the weeds getting belligerent. That is why this chapter takes a relaxed view of leaving a few *Toxicodendron* shrubs around the edges if there is room for them. As long as they don't get out of hand, one or two stuck away in the back 40 will keep you on your toes. They provide a reason to suspect they are on the move and prepare you for sneak attacks. And, admit it, they are pretty in fall. In addition to the sources cited below, it was a particular pleasure to talk with a few experts in this specialty.

Olkowski, William, Sheila Daar, and Helga Olkowski, *Common-Sense Pest Control* (Newtown, CT, Taunton Press, 1991).

Seymour, B.S.A., ed., *The Wise Garden Encyclopedia* (New York, Wm. H. Wise & Co., 1954).

University of California Cooperative Extension, *Poison Oak Control in the Home Garden* (Leaflet 2573, Jul. 1976).

Periodicals

Cox, Jeff, "Eradicating Poison Ivy from Land and Body," *Organic Gardening & Farming*, Jun. 1976, pp. 94-96.

Daar, Sheila, "Safe Ways to Outwit Poison Ivy and Poison Oak," *Common Sense Pest Control Quarterly*, Volume 7, No. 4, 1991, pp. 7-14.

Tapley, George Otis, "Cities Can Destroy Poison Ivy: Brookline, Massachusetts, Has Found an Effective, Safe Method," *American City*, Aug. 1944, pp. 53, 117.

Fine Gardening, "Getting Rid of Poison Oak & Ivy," Jul./Aug. 1993, p. 12.

Popular Science, "Good Riddance to Rhus Toxicodendron: Chemical Warfare against Plant Nuisance No. 1," Jun. 1944, pp. 162-163.

Popular Science, "Outwit Poison Ivy," Jul. 1953, pp. 116-120.

CHAPTER NINE: Parting Words

Ending at the beginning is an old trick, but there was also enough information to allow it. We deny a West Coast bias and attribute our circularity to taking our narrative where the facts were. There may be plenty of like data in local archives elsewhere, and we probably could have started and ended in Masachusetts, Michigan, or Mississippi. In which event, we rest our case. Poison ivy and oak have ever dogged Americans' steps like a hopeful stray. What happened in California is exemplary and perhaps didactic. Play this chapter locally and fill in your own names and places. Our sources for it are:

Hagwood, Joseph J., Jr., *The California Debris Commission: A History* (Sacramento, CA, Sacramento District U.S. Army Corps of Engineers, 1981).

Killam, Jack, *Ballads of the Poison Oak* (San Diego, CA, Commercial Press, 1927).

McPhee, John A., *Assembling California* (New York, Farrar, Straus and Giroux, 1993).

Stuart, Malcolm, ed., *The Encyclopedia of Herbs and Herbalism* (New York, Crescent Books 1987 [© 1979]).

Ullman, Dana, *Homeopathy: Medicine for the 21st Century* (Berkeley, CA, North Atlantic Books, 1988).

INDEX

MAIN ENTRIES for plant species other than those of the Toxicodendron are their common English names unless, like many foreign species, they lack one common name. Then the Latin binomial is the main entry.

A

Alcohol
  See Organic solvents
Allergenic extracts 79-82
  deaths from 81
  FDA withdrawal order 82
  maintenance dose 79
  nearly fatal 9
  side effects 81
  U.S. Army 79
Allergies
  percent population with 6, 60
Allergy attack 47-58
  cell fluid 54
  chemotaxis 53
  cytolysis 54
  delayed hypersensitivity 57

grace period 48
lymphokines 53
not contagious 54
repeated sensitizing exposures 48
sensitizing contact 47
T "memory" cells 56
time, sensitivity over 48
urushiol dermatitis 53
Aluminum acetate
  See Drugs, OTC
American Smoke Tree 92
  Cotinus obovatum
  Chittam wood
Americans, Native, uses of poison ivy, etc.
  baskets 14-15
  food 14-15

Extracts, allergenic
  See Allergenic extracts

F

Florida Holly
  See Brazilian Pepper Tree
Florida Poisonwood Tree
  Metopium toxifera 89
Franklin, Benjamin 22
French, Sanford William 79

G

Gibbons, Euell 77
Gillis, William T. 30, 34, 86, 107
Ginkgo Tree
  Ginkgo biloba 91
Gloves
  cotton, leather 11, 98
  rubber 11
  for eradication 98
Goat milk
  See Resistance
Goats
  for eradication 104
  dairy 104
  Spanish and angora 104
Graham, Hugh 80
Granulocytes 53
Gronovius, Johann Friedrich 20
Guin, Jere D., M.D. 81

H

Haptens 50
Hennen, Joe 30
Herbicides
  2,4-D 102
  best time to apply 103
  glyphosates 102
  triclorpyls 102

Hog Gum
  See Florida Poisonwood Tree
Hollister-Stier Laboratories 80
Home remedies 65-71
  astringents 66
  bicarbonate of soda 73
  jewelweed 67
  list of 65
  oats 72
  placebo effect 71
  plantain 66
  Steam baths 69
  vinegar 73
  water, very hot 73
Hooker, Sir William Jackson 26
Horsfield, Thomas, M.D. 54
Hudson's Bay Company 26

I

IgG 52, 79, 83
Immune response 51-54
  antibodies 52
  antigens 48
  B cells 52
  B memory cells 52
  chemotaxis 53
  granulocytes 53
  haptens 50
  IgG 52
  immunoglobulins 52
  leukocytes 52
  macrophages 53
  neoantigens 49
  normal flora 48
  pathogens 48
  phagocytes 53
  receptor molecules 53
  stem cells 52
  T cells 52
  T helper cells 53

Also from

Acton Circle...

Lawn Care & Gardening: A down-to-earth guide to the business,
by Kevin Rossi

Successful lawn care and gardening can be a fulfilling job that demands all of a person's business and technical abilities. While no one volume can contain everything about this engrossing and rewarding occupation, *Lawn Care & Gardening: A down-to-earth guide to the business* gets the reader off on the right foot, provides a solid core of information, and leads easily to more.

It covers the technical details of management and gardening better than any other book on the subject and does it in a lively, personal manner.

Learn about—

- Building a base of satisfied paying customers, scheduling and managing the workload, and being an employer
- Tools and equipment, how to judge their quality and where to find them
- The legal requirements for starting the business
- The essentials for a simple bookkeeping system
- The chemistry of soils, fertilizers, and plant growth, as well as the best way to mow lawns, prune shrubbery, encourage plants, and discourage pests

"an excellent and efficient general guide for beginners"
—George Cohen, *Booklist*

"an important title for horticultural entrepreneurs"
—Diane C. Donovan, *The Bookwatch*

Order Information